THE SNUFF TAKER'S EPHEMERIS

Volume Five

Spring 2012

© 2012, Lucien Publishing.

THE SNUFF TAKER'S EPHEMERIS is published sporadically by Lucien Publishing, Fayetteville NC. Volume Five, Spring 2012. Cost: 9.99/single volume; 39.96/per year. Address: PO Box 287, Spring Lake, NC 28390. www.STephemeris.com.

Advertising and distribution/bulk purchase queries: distribution@STephemeris.com.

ISBN-13: 978-0985478100

ISBN-10: 0985478101

Contents

WHAT THE HELL HAPPENED TO THIS MAGAZINE?

Good question.

In case you haven't noticed, our format has changed wildly.

We're bigger than ever before- both figuratively and literally. Our size has increased from the paltry 5x9 digest size to a whopping 8x10. While we've been wanting to go big for a while now, it was something of a must considering our new distribution deal. For the first time ever, we're now available at most major book stores, both online and brick and mortar. At our old size, we were almost invisible behind those tall newsstand backers, and we definitely don't rate front-of-rack placement like *Reader's Digest* or *Jet*, so we had to boost the overall dimensions in order to be seen.

We've also been guilty of squeezing in fine print on some of our articles in order to get as much info into each issue as possible. With our new giant format, we're able to keep all of our type at 11 points and higher. Tell your eyes that they're welcome.

But this new format is not without its disadvantages. First, we had to increase our cover price from 8.83 to 9.99. We know the extra buck is painful, but for the added features and increased circulation, we think most of our readers will understand. Secondly, we've gone from a full color to a black and white interior. This was the most agonizing choice we had to make, but we wanted to keep the cover price as low as possible. Adding color would have almost doubled the price with our current page count. We had the option of either cutting down to 50 pages or dropping the color, and we chose the latter. (Our e-copies, of course, will remain full-color).

Aside from the facelift, The Ephemeris' content will remain as awesome as it ever was, probably even *more* awesome, if that can be believed. We're still the same snotty, anti-establishment history buffs that we always were. There's just more of us to love now.

RW HUBBARD

Mick Hellwig

Letters

STE,

Love your magazine. What a nice unpretentious read!

I do however, as a Canadian gun owner, take some exception with the Crazy Cat Lady's article in STE #2. Canada has a fairly high rate of gun ownership. 13th highest in the world, in fact. Canadians can indeed own handguns, and own hundreds of thousands of them, if not millions. Long guns are very common, as is hunting, target shooting, etc.. Many of us participate in action pistol shooting sports, IDPA, IPSC, SASS, PPC etc..

Our gun ownership laws are absolutely draconian however, and the government heavily regulates ownership, transport and storage of firearms. Hopefully this will change, and given recent events, it looks like the government is beginning deregulation. Our long gun registry, long a bone of contention amongst law abiding citizens is due to be abolished in the new year. As gun owners, we hope it is the first of many changes towards liberty and freedom, much like our American cousins enjoy.

As a nose stuffer and pipe smoker, I absolutely love your magazine. Please keep up the good work, and I will continue to be a faithful reader.

Cheers,
Kolya Ramirez-Hughes

Thanks for writing in, Kolya! It's always great to hear from a fellow North American freedom enthusiast.

Jennifer has been known to exaggerate from time to time in order to prove a point. She once told me that her husband made her so angry that she stabbed him in the leg with a screwdriver. (Turns out it was just an ink pen). Speaking of Jennifer:

sTe,

I've noticed that Jennifer Goldsmith's articles have been missing for the last couple of issues. She is, I hope, still writing for STE?

Dan Blaine,
Colorado

Yes, Jen is still with us. Here's her excuse for being absent: "I've just been really, really busy and really, really lazy. I've got articles I need to finish but my day job keeps getting in the way. But I shall return as soon as I get my poop in a group." Make sure you check out her movie review this issue.

Dear Ephemeris,

I've been thinking back to my favorite articles from the last few issues and I realized they all were written by Micah Rimel. Who is this guy and where can I find more of his work?

Cheers,
Anonymouse

Like most of our writers, Micah is knee-deep in other stuff when he's not busy editorially managing us or writing about snuff. Aside from his burgeoning stand-up comedy act and live music career, Micah has been helping to keep Austin weird by peering in through the windows of mobile home residents hoping to see "something cool." We're all very proud of his voyeuristic accomplishments. His wife, understandably, is not.

Obligatory Hate Mail Department

Note: We've not altered this letter in N E wayz.

Ha ha ha, real f#ing funny. Let's be a cliched hipster and take an old fifties training film and redub it to a modern era. **[We're still trying to wrap our heads around that sentence, but we believe the author is referencing our youtube video, "The Terrible Truth About Smokeless Tobacco."]** Except you aren't funny in the least. You make fun of the rigtheous argument against tobacco by making it to appear that those who oppose the deadly think are stupid or backwards. I'll have you to know that I lost 2 uncles to throat cancer from dipping and you know what, evne though you guys are evil assholes I wouldn't for one moment wish that apon you. Because it is a horrible death.

Saying that spit tobacco isn't dangeroue is like saying that its ok to hold a posionous snake. You are literally playing with fire and I sure hope you book doesn't fall into the hands of miners because they'll think that its ok to do snuss and dip snuff. **[We agree 100%. Miners are terribly impressionable people, and we would hate to for them to inhale deadly snuff instead of coal dust.]** Just think twice guys when you say something because you never know whose listening. Laterz.

"Brandy"
Via youtube

Well, now we know where that one "dislike" came from.

Dearest Ephemeris,

As someone who has been with the book since issue one, I'm starting to notice a bit of right-wing paranoia beginning to creep into the magazine. I know that most of your staff consider yourselves to be libertarian, but in the classical sense of the word doesn't that just mean that you're a conservative with a broader outlook than what the republican party has to offer?

Just hoping my favorite magazine doesn't go all Newt Gingrich on me.

TS,
Florida

T, thanks for writing. I wouldn't say that "most of our staff" is libertarian. Aside from myself (RW Hubbard), only Jennifer Goldsmith and James Walter identify themselves as libertarian. (And Jen doesn't count, since she's in Canada.)

Other than that, we have a couple of liberals on staff as well as a few conservatives. The only other person I can think of that has actually stated that they belong to any particular party is Bill Johnson, who is a dyed-in-the-wool southern democrat ("But not the Lyndon Johnson kind,"* he says,* "the good kind.")

The Ephemeris is NOT a libertarian magazine, nor is it a tool of the left, right or center wing. We believe here that adults should be free to use whatever tobacco products they wish to use without government interference of any kind. That makes us enemies of pretty much every politician in the world and half of society to boot, so don't think we're playing favorites.

Letter of the Month

Are you masochists? I get the impression that you are all a bunch of self loathing hipsters in tight jeans. Every mean spirited, berating letter sent to you from some worthless, over-educated, pompous degenerate who values their opinions above all others is immediately praised, published and rewarded. Either this is blatant bribery or you love to have others join in on the mocking of your publication, which is something you seem to take great pleasure in. I hope you do not let these fools who spew their petty complaints to no end, and take offense to the most minute of all details have any influence on your decisions. I see no constructiveness in their criticism most likely because their brains are mired in the self-righteous filth they secrete.

I was caught off guard when my favorite columnist, Bill Johnson, was labeled a chauvinistic, racist coot. This critic's ignorance shone clear at this moment- it lifted from the page like poisonous vapours that caused my brain to convulse and nearly lead to the spontaneous release of my bowels. For one to judge a man (a veteran, no less) from a generation she was not a part of is very telling of her character. I would guess this hasty moral critiquing stems from a false sense of supremacy. I hope the following generation will not be so quick to judge the previous by the cultural changes that no doubt will occur in the future.

Now allow me to be a hypocrite. I am inclined to think that your staff favours (or at least, at the moment) snus to snuff. Perhaps it's your new infatuation, perhaps it's your old standby; either way, it reflects in your publication. I do not take snus nor have I ever, the temptation someday may very well overtake me but for the time being I am content with my existing vices. That being said I cannot identify with the articles pertaining to it, that isn't to say that I don't find them interesting. I understand that snus and snuff are cousins of sorts and a great deal of people use both. It causes me no great grief but I would enjoy a larger ratio of snuff articles.

The short stories were a bit of a surprise. I was not sure if I liked the idea but after reading them both I am forced to admit I do. The first was very well written and it bared great resemblance to O. Henry's classic Ransom of Red Chief. It

was a great read with clever analogies- well done, sir.

The latter was cut from a more modern cloth and showed great potential as you stated. I would not mind in the least reading either one of these authors works again. I would encourage you to feature them in the future.

In closing, I love your sleaze rag- it is my sleaze rag of choice. I enjoyed your first two issues very much and the third was no exception. Your next will be wonderful, I am sure, as long as there is plenty of Bill Johnson. I wish you all the success you lazy bastards can muster.

Your friendly neighborhood interdimensional drainpipe navigator,

Beaver
Morrisville, NC

Despite our tight jeans, porkpie hats and John Waters moustaches, we don't consider ourselves to be hipsters, but we sure enjoy hearing that folks either love us or hate us. A strong reaction, no matter how bad, beats the hell out of a neutral response any day. But just so you don't go getting the impression that we only reward readers that hate us, we've chosen your epistle as the letter of the month. Congratulations on your free one-year subscription, you brown-nosing SOB!

I'll be the first to admit that I favor Swedish snus over nasal snuff, but I like to think that I'm balanced out by Mick (who prefers snuff to snus) and Micah (who exclusively uses snuff). On the other hand, our motto (one of them, anyway) is that "it's all snuff" and at the end of the day a tin of WoS Strasbourg can hold hands with a tin of Copenhagen while getting a backrub from Göteborg's Rapé. But we will try to balance our content a little better in the future, so stick around.

Speaking of the snus/snuff conflict:

Dear STE,

I'm seeing now that you're dropping all the snuff advertisements from the book in favor of snus. All the small company ads are being replaced with ads from giant tobacco conglomerates. Is there any particular reason for this change in marketing?

David Howell,
Reno Nevada

David, we haven't "dropped" any advertisers from the book, be they snuff or snus makers. We'll run an ad from any legitimate company, big or small, who offers a service or manufactures a product we like and use.

As you may well know, many snuff manufacturers operate on teeny, tiny budgets and most don't have a great deal of advertising dollars to spend, even at our modest rates. And while we'd like to be able to donate free ad space for all the companies we love, it would be unfair to the advertisers who do *purchase ad space from us.*

Dear friends,

I recently read where [someone] criticized you for putting "political propaganda" in the STE. What kind of fantasy world does he live in? This administration has been particularly hard on smokeless tobacco users in the US. Mail order bans, FDA shackles on reduced harm tobacco products, flavoring bans, giant warning labels, unprecedented tax increases, advertising restrictions and keeping a giant database of every person who has ever purchased or inquired about tobacco over the internet– these are all things that are going on right now and have affected almost every single person who reads your magazine. It would be in poor taste for you to **not** mention politics in the STE, especially when they threaten the freedoms that we all cherish.

My husband and I appreciate that you feature a rundown on all the new litigation that faces us each issue. We don't frequent any tobacco news groups and the one [smokeless tobacco] forum that we visit regularly doesn't allow political discussion. It also happens to be full of the sheeple that claim you're "condescending" and "political". These sheeple are probably descended from the Colonial Americans who couldn't understand why the Patriots would rebel against such a nice king, or maybe from the Europeans who sat by and let Hitler stuff 10 million people into ovens because they didn't want to "involve themselves in political discussions."

In all, we just wanted to say thanks for being a welcome anecdote to the pompous, self-righteous assholes that seem to frequent [snuff forums]. Keep telling us about the naked emperor, in all his unclothed glory, while the rest of the world buries its head in the sand.

Kagan Spilisy
via internet

Kagan, how dare you mention the 900 pound elephant in the room! Don't you know that our readers prefer us to write about the mythical dreamland we all live in where snuff users are free from governmental prosecution? Shame on you! Next you're going to tell us that babies don't come from storks or that Prince Adam is the secret identity of He-Man. Nonsense!

All kidding aside, while we hate coming across like blowhards, there are some hobbies you should probably not take up if you wish to avoid political discourse of any kind. Tobacco is third on the list, after guns and abortion. (Speaking of which, we wish to take this opportunity to mention our newest companion title, Abortion & Ammo Monthly. *We expect it to sell well in the Middle East.)*

That's it for this issue, kids. Stop all the downloading and send us a note at letters@STephemeris.com *or PO Box 287, Spring Lake NC 28390.*

Laterz.

Ephemera!

... collecting all the news that's fit to reprint

Stan Glantz at it again

Stanton Glantz, director of The Center for Tobacco Control (USoC), has long been a foe of reduced-harm tobacco consumption. A subscriber to the notion that "if you can't attack the science, you should misconstrue it or attack the source," Glantz published an article criticizing the *New York Times* and *USA Today* for running pieces on Brad Rodu and Riccardo Polosa's recent smoke cessation study.

The study, which is making headlines around the world, reveals nothing new that decades of similar studies haven't already shown: smokeless tobacco is at least 98% safer than cigarette smoking, and smokeless tobacco products are ~80% more effective at helping smokers quit than pharmaceutical alternatives.

But this data doesn't sit well with Stan Glantz, who wishes to ban all tobacco use no matter how harmless. Glantz attacks the mainstream media for "uncritically" accepting the data in Rodu's study, and goes on to suggest that since Rodu's research is backed by the tobacco industry, it is somehow inaccurate or misrepresented.

Glantz then chastises *USA Today* for not "mention[ing] all the evidence of bias in industry funded studies." But in a stunning display of hypocrisy, he then cites the Dec. 12 study by anti-tobacco funded Dept. Of Preventative Medicine (UTN) that he claims shows that smokeless tobacco use is a "gateway drug" that leads to harder cigarette smoking. (In the study, a group of smokeless tobacco-using Air Force recruits were deprived of their snuff and presented with cigarettes instead. Not surprisingly, most of them opted for cigarettes rather than go cold turkey.)

But that's not all! Glantz goes on to cite the famous Swedish Snus 30-year "construction worker study" that shows snus users are at no significantly higher risk for heart disease or cancer than non-users. But instead, he misinterprets the data to show that "snus users are at a doubled risk for heart failure than non-users." Technically, it's true. 1 out of 100 non-snus users died of heart failure. 2 out of 100 snusers died of heart failure. (The rates for pancreatic cancers were the same: 1/100 for non-users, 2/100 for snusers). Anyone in the medical or scientific field knows that 1% is never a significant percentage in terms of epidemiological studies.

You would think that someone with a Ph.D would know better. This means that either Stan Glantz is stupid, or a liar. Regardless, we don't like him.

New Study Finds Camel Snus Higher in TSNAs than Marlboro Snus

An abstract published by Oxford American reveals that (American) Camel Snus contains more Tobacco Specific Nitrosamines than its Marlboro counterpart. Of all the products tested, dissolvable Camel Orbs and Sticks contained the least amount of TSNAs.

More interestingly, the study found that there existed "significant, regional" differences in the nicotine and TSNA counts in the American snus products. Camel Snus purchased in the south, for example, contained almost three times the amount of nicotine than the same product purchased north of the Mason-Dixon line. (TSNA counts varied almost as wildly as the Nicotine content).

Does this mean that PM and RJR are intentionally manufacturing different varieties of their snus products in order to appease local markets? Phone calls to both companies have yet to be returned.

FDA Studies Not Up To Snuff, Claim Researchers, Chantix Increases Suicide Risks

Smokers trying to quit with Pfizer's nicotine-cessation drug Chantix (called Champix in Europe) are eight times more likely to commit suicide, a new study reports.

In response to overwhelming evidence by earlier studies that showed Chantix to be the major contributor to severe cases of depression and suicide, the FDA launched two independent studies that contradicted the earlier findings. These FDA studies were in turn ripped apart by the scientific community.

According to Dr. Curt Furburg, "Our study contradicts the implications of a recent review by the FDA showing no difference in psychiatric hospitalizations between varenicline and nicotine replacement patches." Furburg is professor of Public Health Sciences at Wake Forest Baptist Medical Center, co-author of the study published online in the Public Library of Science journal PLoS One.

"The FDA hospitalization studies were flawed because they could not capture most of the serious psychiatric side effects, including suicide, depression, aggression and assaults. These can be catastrophic events but do not normally result in hospitalization," Furberg said in a statement.

The FDA later acknowledged that their studies were flawed. "The scope of the studies [was] too narrow and didn't include independent incidents that took place outside of the hospital."

In contrast, the PLoS One study reported that almost 90% of Chantix users suffered from depression and/or suicidal thoughts. Even more disturbingly, less than 10% of Chantix users successfully stop smoking for longer than a year.

How is it that such an unsafe drug is being promoted by the FDA while relatively harmless smokeless tobacco risks being outlawed? Consider that over the last decade, the Federal Government has reaped over 10 billion dollars from Pfizer (not to mention an approximate 12 million dollars of lobbyist cash paid to various Republo-crat candidates) and the fact that the FDA can promote steadily increasing tobacco taxes in the guise of "public health", it would appear that the government is attempting to have its cake and eat it, too; all at the cost of our health and well-being.

"F. You" from the EU: How Three Men Managed To Keep Moist Snuff Banned in Europe

Sweden's hope of removing the export ban on snus appeared to be crushed this past summer. The EU Commission announced that most member countries support the ban wholeheartedly. But our review shows that in fact there is strong support for marketing snus freely, all across Europe.

"A majority of member countries prohibit all forms of oral tobacco, including snuff," announced the European Commission in July. The basis for the statement came from a "public consultation" on tobacco laws. It garnered 85,000 responses to the questions on snuff, snus, tobacco advertising and the appearance of cigarette packs.

EU Health Commissioner John Dalli made clear shortly thereafter that the Commission (comprised of himself and two of his friends) had already decided to continue the export ban on snus.

But the results of the consultation appeared only in the last month, and a review of these petitions gives a very different result.

More than eight out of ten citizens, 84 percent, support lifting of the ban on snus. 86 percent of government representatives and 74 percent of industry representatives also wish to lift the ban. The only group polled that wish to continue the smokeless tobacco ban was a small group of lobbyists- and among them, only 56% voted to keep the ban.

The EU Commission rejected, however, 99% of the responses on the grounds that "two-thirds are from Italy and Poland, where tobacco merchants organized petition drives." But even if we exclude these two countries, the majority voted to lift the export ban on snus, 10-6, when respondents are broken down by country.

Spokesperson Frederic Vincent defends the Commission's opposing statement that only took into account the government representatives who responded: "The report is based on a qualitative analysis based on responses from Member States, ie, governments and ministries."

But our review of the 400 responses in this group show that even among the responses from parliamentarians, municipalities, government agencies and ministries that 71 percent voted to lift the export ban.

The European Commission's health directorate claims to have received responses from governments in support of the ban on snus, but refuses to show them.

Snus manufacturer Swedish Match accuses the European Commission of trying to sweep the snus issue under the rug. "These are very strange conclusions that the Commission drew from the results, which of course shows strong support for the lifting of the ban," says communications director Patrick Hildingsson.

In Sweden, all political parties oppose the ban on snus and Minister for Trade Ewa Björling (M) has raised the issue as a breach of the EU internal market rules. But the EU ban on snus has been introduced for health reasons and therefore it is Minister of Health for the Young and Elderly, Maria Larsson (Christian Democrats), that will represent Sweden in the forthcoming negotiations on tobacco legislation. However, Maria Larsson's political advisor Ulrik Lindgren says that the minister "Is not following the issue very closely."

Originally reported 11-30-11 by Henrik Bors for Dagens Nyheter.

India: Comparative Risk Study Shows Dry Snuff To Be Safest Choice Among Smokeless Tobacco Products

A recent study in Bangladesh concluded that snuff takers in Southeast Asia face the same statistical risk of heart disease as their western counterparts; that is to say, no increased risk whatsoever.

The study focused on non-smoking users of guthka, gul, and dry snuff between the ages of 40-75. Guthka and gul are two types of creamy moist snuff sold in squeeze tubes similar to toothpaste. (Guthka, a combination of tobacco, clove and beetle nut, has been found to be highly carcinogenic. Gul, which is manufactured from sugar, molasses and tobacco, has not been known to cause the same high rates of oral cancer experienced by guthka users).

The authors of the report concluded that "there was no statistically significant association between smokeless tobacco use in general and heart disease among non-smoking adults in Bangladesh."

The report did find, however, that the heart disease rate among gul users was statistically higher than that of users of other forms of smokeless tobacco.

"Truth" Campaign: On Its Last Legs?

The American Legacy Foundation, svengalies behind the often-ridiculed "Truth" campaign, are running out of money.

The ALF was funded in 1998 as a way to appropriate part of the $206 billion dollars the federal government had just taken from the tobacco industry. The idea was to make a series of youth-targeted ads that espoused the dangers of cigarette smoking.

Memorable TV ads feature staged scenes such as a group of teenagers dumping thousands of body bags in front of "Big Tobacco" headquarters in order to demonstrate the number of smoking related causalities caused by the evil corporations.

With cigarette smoking on the decline, Truth set its sights on smokeless tobacco, grossly misrepresenting the associated risks and accusing snuff makers of targeting teens and children.

But now they're running out of money. At one time, their media budget was estimated at $200 million a year, compared to the $32 million spent in 2009. The Legacy Foundation is currently seeking federal funding in order to continue their smear campaign of lies and misinformation.

Bhutanese Monk Gets Three Years in Prison for Smokeless Tobacco

The tiny republic of Bhutan, the first nation in the modern world to completely ban the sale and public use of all tobacco products, has successfully prosecuted its first offender under the new law.

24 year old Buddhist monk Sonam Tshering was caught carrying 46 single packets of Baba brand chewing tobacco (the estimated total gross

street value: $2.50) and sentenced to three years in federal prison.

Even supporters of the new law find the sentence incredibly harsh and undeserving. You can voice your opinion to the Bhutan Royal Court of Justice by contacting them directly at **judiciary@druknet.bt**. At the time of this writing, 65 Bhutanese have been jailed for possessing tobacco.

American Snuff Products: Now Safer Than Ever?

TSNA levels in USST products (both moist and dry snuff) have dropped by over half since 1997.

According to a recent study by Altria, the levels of nitrosamines in their smokeless tobacco products have continuously dropped each consecutive year since the early 1980s, to a level that is now comparable to some Swedish snus brands.

The study also confirms that American manufacturers made drastic changes to the way in which they process their smokeless tobacco crops. By 2005, the US Smokeless Tobacco Company- makers of such brands as Skoal, Copenhagen and Red Seal- had refined their fermentation process to the point that bacterial TSNA did not increase after manufacture, meaning that the TSNAs in the finished product were initially present in the raw crop and not a byproduct of lackluster and outdated production methods.

This puts USST "dip" brands roughly in the same category as the few lower-tiered Swedish snus manufacturers that still use the traditional psuedo-fermentation process.

Now that smokeless manufacturers in the US have attained the level of sophistication that the Swedes reached over 40 years ago, perhaps we can anticipate air cured and steam-pasteurized American snuff products by the year 2052.

PACT Act Tax Collection Temporarily Blocked

Federal Judge Royce Lamberth (D-Washington DC) blocked provisions in the PACT Act that require internet or mail-order vendors from collecting out of state sales taxes.

Citing the tax collection provision as a violation of constitutional due rights, Lamberth said that the "enforcement of a potentially unconstitutional law that would also have severe economic effects is not in the public interest."

Unfortunately, Lamberth upheld the ban on tobacco shipments through the USPS, claiming it curbed underage tobacco use.

BY THE NUMBERS:

Number of Americans that have tried the following alternative tobacco products:

Snus: 7.7 million
Hookah: 12.2 million
E-Cigs: 3.7 million
Dissolvables: 1 million

Source: American Academy of Pediatrics

Despite Higher Prices, Smokeless Tobacco Sales on the Rise In Convenience Stores

In a December interview with *Convenience Store Decisions*, St. Louis-based C-Store owner Amer Hawatmeh claims that his stores are relying heavily on smokeless tobacco sales due to a dwindling cigarette market and attractive prices for smoke-free alternatives.

The recent launch of the Skoal Blend line has been a huge success. "It's all under $3 for a can. You're seeing that the chewers—the guys who were buying the roll for $5 a can—are switching to this line because when you go from $5 to $3, that's a nice savings," he said. "And it's the same product line with the same name on the can. It's just called Skoal Blend."

Hawatmeh also bemoaned the disappointing sales of NRT products: "One of the things that we aimed to do was bring in all the nicotine chews and other cessation products for all the people trying to stop smoking, but we were just getting stuck with inventory. The consumer who wants to smoke is going to smoke," Hawatmeh said. "I thought sales of tobacco substitutes would go through the roof, especially when you're competing against the big-box guys who are trying to get a bigger margin on it. It just wasn't working for us."

But Hawatmeh was less than enthusiastic about possible forthcoming government restrictions on snuff items: "Every day somebody gets a new itch and they create a new law, and every law seems aimed at prohibiting us from selling tobacco to adult consumers." Preach on, Brother Amer. We hear you.

Swedish Match branches out into Canada and Eurasia; Launches Several New Products

At the February 2012 Snus Summit held in New York City, Swedish Match unveiled a slew of new SKU's, most of them intended for the burgeoning Canadian, Eastern European and Asian markets.

General Smooth, **PSWL**, **Mint/Fresh**, and **Titanium** (left, top to bottom) will be available in Canada next month and are of a smaller pouch design than traditional SM portions. If you live outside of Canada and are unable to locate these new flavors, don't worry; they're the same products available in Europe and the US, just packaged under a new name. (If you're trying to figure out what **General Titanium** is- it's actually **Onyx**.) The same rebranding applies to most of the other following products:

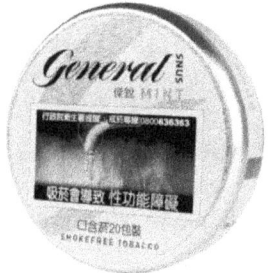

General Original and **Fresh** (Upper right): Central Asia, Southeast Asia

Marlboro Original and **Mint** (Lower right): Central Asia

Parliament Mint, **Intense**, and **Original** (Bottom): Eastern Europe

All of the above listed brands will be packaged in the same metal can as the soon-to-be-discontinued **General Smooth**.

continued

In other Swedish Match news:

- **Göteborg's Rapé** will be getting a limited "Äre Edition" can. **(4)**

- **General Mini Strong**, a new addition to the mini line, will be released this month. **(3)**

- **General Long Portion Extra Strong,** a new, high nicotine snus is headed your way soon.

- **General Onyx's** trademark black portion material recently turned white. Apparently, everyone hates the new look, so Onyx will be back in black starting next month.

- **Nick and Johnny Radical Red** has already made its debut. The "Xtra Strong Chili Snus" rounds out the recently revamped N&J line, which now consists of **Original Edge**, **White Heat**, and **Crushed Ice**.

- The **Lab Series** line gets a slight makeover. For reasons unknown, **01** cans will be sporting big yellow letters instead of black.

- The **Catch** line has been completely redesigned (yet again). The full-sized **Eucalyptus** and **Licorice** sport the plain-jane 80's style wrappers also seen on the mini-sized **Dry Eucalyptus**, **Dry Licorice**, and **Licorice Mini**. The limited edition, spearmint flavored **Lafayette Street** doesn't carry the new look, however. (And for those wondering why all of SM's mini portions except the Catch brand sport the new slim-line can, we were told that the Dry-style portions exclusive to the Catch line are incompatible with the new slim-can packaging machinery. So there you go.)

- If you haven't heard, the **Kronan Portion** cans now come equipped with the standard catch/disposal lid on top. Thank God.

- Beginning this month, all of Swedish Match's snus cans will feature the three-star logo that SM has used since 1969. **(1)**

- The tobacco-free **Onico** line will be getting a fresh publicity push, including television commercials to be broadcast in Norway.

- Though it reportedly did well in some regions, the US test marketing of **Ettan Snuff** is no more. Let's hope they try again in the near future.

- The extremely limited edition **Kardus** brand, handmade by "little old ladies" at the Stockholm Tobacco Museum, gets two new additions to the line. For the first time ever, **Göteborg's Rapé** and **Göteborg's Prima Fint** will bear the Kardus name, meaning that they will be manufactured using the original, late 18th century recipes and natural ingredients common to that era. Also available will be the perennial favorites **Grov** and **Ettan**. Expect to find less than 100 packages of each for sale worldwide... **(2)**

- We're less than happy to report Swedish Match's most recent portion-shrinkage. The new standard weight for traditional portions is 0.9 grams, down ten percent from 1 gram. Lös cans will be losing 3 grams- down from 45g to 42g. Swedish Match claims that this is a cost cutting measure in face of increased Swedish taxation. "Consumers will barely notice it," claims an overly optimistic Patrik Hildingsson.

①

②

③

④

Frederick Tranter, a Fond Farewell

It would appear that the "Freddy T" brand is no more.

Dating back to 1898, the Frederick Tranter company (like many British snuffs) began to fall on hard times during the 1980s and their snuff production rights were purchased by Wilsons of Sharrow. (Two brick and mortar tobacconists shops bearing the Frederick Tranter name remained, though sadly only one exists today).

By the 1990s, the Tranter brand was just a label. All of the snuffs sold under the FT name were re-branded Wilsons flavors, and it appeared that WoS was keeping the label alive simply for nostalgia's sake.

A source close to Wilsons confirmed that they were shutting down production of the Frederick Tranter brand, citing sluggish sales and a lack of brand familiarity among all but the most dedicated snuffers. "When they find out that they can get the same recipe [under the Wilson's name], the average Tranter customer usually seeks out the Wilson's version, which is much easier to find, and probably cheaper to boot."

It is unclear whether WoS will keep or sell the production rights to the Tranter brand, or if it is possible that the FT tobacco shop could begin producing snuff under the Tranter name in the future. But for all intents and purposes, the Frederick Tranter line is dead and gone.

Gotland Newspaper Names Gotlandssnus AB "Company of the Year" For 2011

In recognition for ten years of hard work and outstanding service, *Foretagarna* named Gotlandssnus AB "Business of the Year" and owner Henrik Jakobsson "Entrepreneur of the Year". Congrats Henrik and Jimmy! Now where's our Flader lös?

No More Timberwolf Rewards Program

If you're a user of Timberwolf Moist Snuff, you better cash in your reward points while there's still time.

Everyone's favorite dope pushers, the FDA, decided in December that Timberwolf customers were taking part in an illegal sweepstakes program and shut it down under the vague auspices of the Tobacco Control Act.

Swedish Match North America, Timberwolf's parent company, in a show of good faith is honoring existing reward points while they still can. In an official statement sent to program participants, SMNA optimistically called the ban "temporary":

"While we do not agree with their decision, we have to temporarily shut down www.TimberWolfSnuff.com while we work with the FDA to resolve this matter."

An inquiry sent to the FDA by the Ephemeris was not immediately returned (it has been 65 days at the time of this writing).

Historic G. Smith & Sons Closes its Doors

For almost 150 years, Smith and Sons of Charing Cross Road was a British institution. At one time considered the world's greatest snuff shop, GS&S carried a full line of tobacco products in addition to their privately blended nasal snuffs.

Even when the popularity of snuff was on the wane, people still frequented the shop just to have a chat with Vivian Rose, who ran Smith and Sons from the 1950's until his death in the late 1980's.

Rose was a one-of-a-kind, curmudgeonly eccentric who took great delight in all facets of snuff-taking, and for decades he served as the unofficial "snuff mascot" to the world media. Vivian Rose was interviewed hundreds of times throughout the course of his career. He never turned down an interview request, and he never tired of talking about snuff.

Sadly, the business changed hands after his passing and longtime customers went away in droves. By all accounts, the new owners had very little knowledge of tobacco in general and proceeded to raise the prices of the store's inventory to the point where Smith and Sons developed a reputation for price gouging.

The knowledgeable, friendly staff with decades of snuff making under their belt had been replaced with surly, belligerent teenagers who could barely speak English. The once-great Snuff Mecca had transformed into nothing more than a corner convenience store- a pale shadow of its former self. Little wonder then that the store shut down this past November, amid no fanfare whatsoever. It deserved so much more than that.

NEW STUFF:
All the fresh products that have launched since last issue

- **Samuel Gawith** Guarana, Hazlenut, Celtic Talisman Aromatic, Plum, Elmo's Reserve, 2011 Christmas Special (SG)

- **Abraxas** Club and Connoisseur Cerise (Abraxas)

- **Dholakia** (ten varieties) (Dholakia)

- **Wilsons** Apricot & Menthol (WoS)

- **The Viking** Brown, Dark, Menthol, Peach, Spear (MSS/SG)

- **Revor** Plug (GH)

- **Grimm & Triepel 150th Anniversary** (seven varieties, traditional chew plugs) (G&T)

- **RMD Guthka** (Manikchand)

- **Supreme Parag Guthka** (Kothari)

- **Rajnigandha Masala** (Dharampal Satyapal)

- **Paul Gotard** Polish Snuff (21 Varieties) (PG)

- **Six Photo** Medicated No. 66 (6 Photo)

- **Chema** Plain (Poschl)

- **Ozona** Anis (Poschl)

- **Thai Herbal** Yellow (TH)

- **STOK Snuff** (ten varieties) (STKP)

- **Limburgertabak** (Kralingse/Molens)

- **Offroad** Coffee Supreme (v2)

- **Thunder** Coola Loose (v2)

- **Nordstrommen** Brandy Alexander and Jule (Re-releases, limited) (v2)

- **Gotland's Julessnus** (Limited Annual Release) (Gotlandssnus)

- **Mocca** Black, Pink & Red (Formerly Licorice, Mint & Pomegranate) (F&L)

- **Mocca Black Maple** "Midi" Portion (F&L)

- **Skruf Slim** Nordic White and Original (Skruf AB)

- **Smalands** White and Original Portions (Skruf AB)

- **Oden's Extreme** Wintergreen (GN)

- **Taboca** White Extra Strong (Taboca)

- **Jakobsson's** Strong Melon (Gotlandssnus)

- **Gringo** Loose (Gringo Snus)

- **Grizzly Premium Natural** (4 varieties) (American Snuff Company)

Note: check the big Swedish Match write-up in this month's Ephemera! *for a comprehensive listing of that company's new items.*

Tragedy Destroys Austin's Fumée Cigars: 17 Dead, 4 Injured

Austin, Texas- A New Year's Eve celebration at Fumée Cigars turned deadly in what witnesses have called "the worst day in Austin's history, except for that one time when Charles Whitman got up on the tower and shot all those people."

Fumée, which billed itself as the "World's Greatest Cigar and Snus Bar," held what was to be an all-night party that began at 6:00 PM on New Year's Eve. But at the same time that billions of people around the world were watching the ball drop in New York's Times Square, the people of Austin were watching a tragedy of errors that would end up claiming the lives of 17 drunken hipsters.

The Ephemeris has been working round the clock to piece the events of that night together, using eyewitness testimony and unsubstantiated rumors to tell the tale of "The Travis County Travesty." A warning: most of what you will read is quite disturbing.

"Lady Heather" and the Russian Mob

According to public record, Fumée (French slang for venereal disease) was owned by a Ukrainian immigrant named Heather Hadstadanvad, known to patrons as "Heather H." or the more ominous "Lady Heather." Raised in an orphanage and smuggled into the United States as part of a sex-trafficking ring during the early 1990's, little is known of Heather's life between then and 2006, when she opened her "Cigar" bar.

Though it would later be called "one of Austin's best kept secrets" by *Jet Blue* magazine, the Fumée of 2006 was a vastly different establishment than the one that would end up burning to the ground. The lobby featured plush, leather chairs and inviting wood decor, but it was merely a front for the private sex rooms in back, where wealthy businessmen were

"Lady" Heather and her accomplice/lover/pimp, "Doktor" Anton Yeded.

lured in with the promise of illicit sexual favors. Heather had a stable of young girls being flown in every week from Eastern Europe, most of them experienced streetwalkers turned brothel whores.

This part of the operation was allegedly run by Heather's former pimp-turned-business partner, Anton Yeded. Rumored to be a defector from the Russian Mob, Yeded was nicknamed "The Doktor" by the girls at Fumée due to his bizarre gynecological fetishes. He would don a ski mask and perform a faux-pap smear on the fully-clothed female "patient" and then demand payment. The girls rarely had money of their own, and Anton would scream at them for hours, berating them, before Heather would finally intervene and make him leave.

Turning Legit

But to the surprise of everyone involved, the counterfeit Cuban cigars being sold at Fumée began making more money than the prostitution ring. Recalls one undocumented Mexican "waitress" who worked there:

"Lady Heather had *cholos* bringing in cheap cigars from Tijuana. They sell for a nickel a stick. But she would put a Cuban label on them and sell them for 50 dollars apiece, and the stupid gringos buy them like they were going out of style 'cause they so stupid. I was like, 'whatever, I'm stealing money out the till every night anyways, so *esta cabrón, puta.*""

By 2008, the boudoirs had been replaced with humidors and the hookers with hookahs. Instead of selling skin, Heather and Anton were selling smoke. Lots of it. It is estimated that 90% of the cigars smuggled out of Mexico in 2007 ended up at Fumée, rebranded to look like expensive Cuban cigars.

But somewhere along the way, Heather ran into problems with her Tijuana connection and she was forced to go completely legitimate, stocking genuine, premium cigars handmade in Central and South America. Friends recall this as a happy time for Heather and Anton. "Anton was supposedly in the process of writing a book about female anatomy, so he was gone most of the time. Heather couldn't have been happier to be by herself. She had affairs with most of the female staff, and once she even held a grand orgy at the bar where people came from all over to take part. Anton came in the next day and was saying 'what's that smell? It smells funny in here' but Heather just said it was leftover from the seafood buffet the night before [*laughs*]!"

And so the fun continued for the next couple of years. Fumée's illicit past was soon forgotten and people came from all over Texas to sample Lady Heather's big brown tubos. Some nights, you could even catch former president George W. Bush at the bar, trying to figure out how to work the cigar cutter. (The staff was always positioned nearby with a box of bandages).

Heather came up with the idea for the first *New Year's Eve at Fumée* celebration, which became something of an annual tradition. The bar would give out free cigars and drinks to happy patrons, keeping them in high spirits while they waited for 12:00 to roll around.

The 2011 party looked to be no different than the ones that came before it. Reservations were sent out and flyers were passed around in parking lots. The scantily-clad bar girl staff stood outside Fumée holding provocative signs with slogans like "Come in and light our fires!" and "Honk if you're horny (for cigars!)" They would call out to passing motorists, in their thick Slavic accents, "Come to bar tonight guys- free wudka and hot dates!"

12/31/11 - 6:00 PM

As the doors opened, people began to pile into the bar. The surveillance footage that survived the fire shows that the crowd was made up mostly of pretentious hipsters, oblivious college jocks and approximately three cigar smokers. All in all, a typical Austin gathering.

8:30 PM

Beyonka Esmerelda, local scenester and noted tumblr blogger, recalls seeing Heather H. purchasing six small yellow pills from a guy wearing a Sega Genesis t-shirt. "I don't know what it was. It didn't look like the Ambien tabs I usually buy. I thought she was buying, like, St. John's Wort or something. You know, to be retro? I don't know."

10:15

Several witnesses notice Heather acting erratically. "Dude," claims Jimbo Hauser, "Chick was tripping *balls*. I mean, she was like blitzed out of her mind! She was running around like, grabbing people's arms and asking them stuff." Hauser does not know exactly what Heather was inquiring of the partygoers. Despite the club's sound system being cranked to its maximum level, Hauser insisted on walking around with his ipod headphones on. "I had spent all day transferring my Charlie Feathers vinyl to CD, and then from CD to mp3. I was rocking out to it, trying to get people to listen to it. His music is so pure... he's like an Appalachian folk poet."

11:30

"That was when it all hit the fan," remembers Tristen Sickle. "I was standing near the bar, with my friend Kate. She was taking a picture of me looking off into the other direction, as if I didn't know I was being photographed." Just then she saw a "foreign" looking man burst through the door, demanding to know who gave his wife drugs.

The man was Anton Yeded, and he was not happy. "He starts going 'I'm Russian Mafia! Blah Blah Blah!' And I thought he was just referencing an obscure Monty Python skit."

Just then, a very disoriented Heather came running towards the front of the bar. "A shark is chasing me," she screamed, "oh my God, a shark is chasing me!" Anton reached out to catch his lover, and inadvertently knocked over a lit hookah that was sitting on top of the bar.

Some of the burning shisha fell out of the waterpipe and into the Tom Collins glass belonging to 33 year old Alamo Drafthouse employee Nate "Beaver" Santaseri. "Ever since he saw it on *Mad Men*, he wanted to go into a bar and order a Tom Collins mix," remembers his girlfriend, Maggie Shay. "Who knew it was going to kill him?"

The drink ignited almost instantly and flames shot upward into Santaseri's face, burning off his muttonchop sideburns. As he frantically tried to keep his horn-rimmed glasses from melting to his face, the sleeves of his polyester suit caught fire. Within seconds, Santaseri's entire body was covered in flames.

As he stumbled around the bar, several patrons unsuccessfully tried pouring Pabst Blue Ribbon on the man in hopes of extinguishing the fire. Nate eventually collapsed into a crowd of pogo-ing psuedo-punks. Most had spray-dyed their hair with ultra-flammable neon coloring, and in less than a minute, half of the club was an inferno.

Fumée's house DJ, MC Superchronik, noticed the flames as they climbed to the ceiling.

Grabbing the mic, he urgently tried to warn the audience. *"The roof! The roof!"* he shouted, *"the roof is on fire!"* The crowd, mistaking his desperate plea for a party anthem, responded that they 'didn't need no water' just as the rafters caved in on them.

Most of the remaining attendees made it out just in time to see the entire structure collapse. All told, the death toll reached 17 that night. Two of those casualties were Heather and Anton, whom many feel are to blame for the whole incident.

Picking up the Pieces

What does the future hold in store for the survivors of the Fumée tragedy? Justice George, who lost two "frienemies" and one "BFF" in the fire, says that he's going to take this opportunity to reflect on the things in life that matter most to him. "William S. Burroughs put it best when he said that fire is a cleanser, like the phoenix rebirthed. Although that's likely more of a figurative rebirth, because the people in the club that burned to death probably weren't experiencing any kind of serendipitous reawakening. They were screaming pretty loud about being on fire."

Sheena Thomas is more concerned about what the loss of Fumée could mean for the city of Austin. "We went to Fumée, like almost every

"It was terrible," recalls fireman Rod Puiller. "Everywhere you looked, there was skinny jeans, fedoras and patterned Keds, just smoldering in the wind. It was hard to fathom that just seconds ago, there had been a douchey emo fag inside those stupid clothes.

"I even saw one kid run back inside to get his knitted cardigan and when he came out, the "World's Greatest Dad" necktie he was wearing got caught in the door. He was screaming for help, but all I could think was 'my daughters got me that very same tie two Christmases ago, and this little prick is wearing it to be ironic'. So ironically, I let him burn to death."

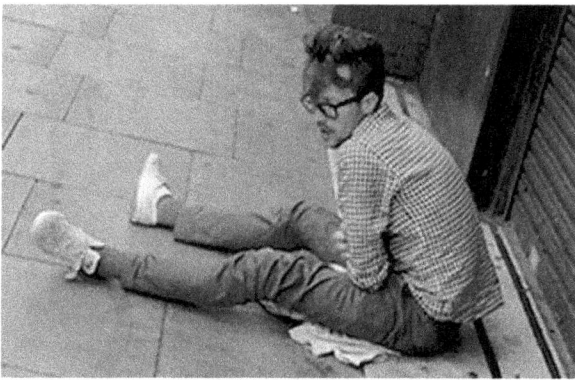

Dazed hipstellectual Robert Armstrong sits outside ground zero waiting for his father to come pick him up. "My fixie had a flat tire," he claimed.

The Fumée Massacre: An Update

As we were going to press with this story, we were contacted by a Mrs. Heather Haddad, who claims to be the public relations spokesperson for Fumée Cigars:

"The details of this story are slightly exaggerated. It is true that Fumée Cigars has closed its doors, and hipsters all over Austin are crying into their matcha tea. I will also concede that a small hookah fire once occurred.

However, we did not deal in the skin trade or counterfeit Cubans. If we had, maybe we would have been more profitable and still in business. Also, everything about "Anton" is true. Thanks for all of the support from our friends at STE." -Heather Haddad

When pressed for further comment, Mrs. Haddad ran away and hid in a small, plastic playhouse.

weekend. I smoke Parliaments during the week, but on the weekend I like to chillax with snus or e-cigs, or whatever I hear is the "in" thing that month. If it wasn't for Fumée, I would have never known that pipe smoking was cool that summer when *Juno* came out, and I would have looked like a total wanker being the only girl in the place without a corncob full of Frog Morton."

If you go to Fumée's website, a simple banner stating "*Fumée Cigars is Permanently Closed*" serves as mute testimony to the atrocities that took place there on New Year's Eve. Scrolling through the site, one can't help but notice the pictures of Eastern European prostitutes posing with lit cigars. Half-nude, 16 year old Belarusian orphans model t-shirts and tank tops imploring one to "Don't just smoke, *Fumée*." It's not hard to understand why so many curious thrill-seekers came to the bar, in search of erotic thrills and so-called "forbidden fruit."

But what can we learn from this massacre? An obvious answer would be that "hookahs and hipsters don't mix." Another would be "stay away from Eurotrash brothels-turned-cigar bars." Other than that, we can't really come up with anything else.

Even though there may not be any kind of deep moral lesson to be gauged from this incident, perhaps the residents of Austin and the survivors of the club tragedy can walk away with a deeper respect for mother nature and her unyielding determination towards ridding the earth of bottom-feeding, parasitic sub-species of genera like the douchebag hipsters who perished in the fire.

STE

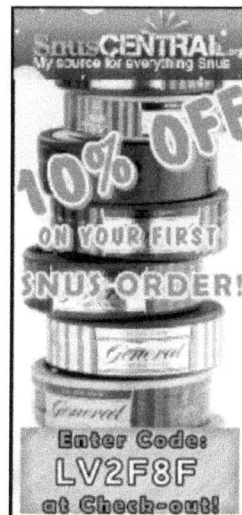

The Wisest Fool In Christendom

Deconstructing King James I, History's First Anti-Tobacco Zealot

By RW Hubbard

2011 marked the 400th anniversary of the first printing of the King James Bible, arguably the most important milestone in publishing history aside from Gutenberg's invention of movable type. But many are unaware that the man that put the Bible into the hands of the common folk also harbored a seething hatred of that era's most prevalent of public vices: tobacco.

Born in 1566 to Mary, Queen of Scots and her cousin James Stewart, Charles James Stewart was named Prince of Scotland shortly after delivery. James never knew either of his parents. Shortly before his son's birth, the elder James had murdered his wife's lover, David Rizzio and was in turn assassinated by Mary's other paramour (and future husband) James Hepburn.

Within a year, his Mother was forced to flee a Protestant rebellion in Scotland and seek asylum under the protection of her cousin Queen Elizabeth I of England. Elizabeth, however suspected Mary to be the source of three earlier assassination attempts on her life and had her imprisoned for nearly 19 years before being executed.

With both of his parents out of the picture, the infant James was named King of Scotland and was delivered to the Earl and Duchess of Mar to be raised at Stirling Castle. He was educated chiefly by the renowned Protestant scholar George Buchanan, who instilled in the young James a love for literature and science.

James (or as he was now known, King James VI of Scotland) began taking an active role in his leadership by the age of 15. He quelled several minor rebellions and soon set his sights on becoming the next king of England. Less than a year after executing his mother, Queen Elizabeth began vetting him as her successor to the throne.

Now 23 years old and amid growing rumors of his suspected homosexuality, James was reluctantly talked into marrying 14 year old Anne of Denmark. Though initially thought to be a marriage of convenience, many believe that James grew to genuinely love his wife. Over time the relationship would produce three surviving children.

His ascension of the English throne in 1604 was not without controversy, as he foiled two different assassination attempts within his first year on the throne. The following year brought with it the notorious Guy Fawkes Gunpowder plot. The resulting publicity regarding this event would endear James to England's Protestant population but would serve to strain relations with both Parliament and the Catholic Church—two political enemies that would trouble James until the end of his reign.

Throughout the rest of his life, James strived to remain popular among his subjects, and to some extent this goal was reached. His manner of taxation, though high, was still less exorbitant than what was levied before his reign. James notably refrained from waging wars and balked at the thought of invading other countries to increase Britain's crown (a fact not lost on his enemies, who were quick to label him a coward.)

In the last decade of his life, James was plagued by several infirmities, among them the gout, arthritis, kidney stones and dementia. His body gradually began to wither away and eventually he would lose all of his teeth. This condition has lead some to conclude that James was suffering from porphyria, a disease which was known to occur in several members of his immediate bloodline.

At this time, he also began to drink heavily which may have contributed to the near-fatal stroke he suffered in early 1625. Two months later, he died of dysentery at the age of 58.

PERSONAL POLICIES

A highly literate man, especially for his era, King James released his first works of poetry at age 19. By 1597 his interests had taken a decidedly more sinister turn and James released an influential exposé on witchcraft entitled *Demonology*.

His interest in the subject was first sparked while visiting his wife's native Denmark and witnessing several native witch hunts. He considered the occult to be a legitimate theological offshoot of Christianity (albeit an evil one) and quickly passed the Scottish Witchcraft Act of 1563, a law which forbade worship of the occult. James personally oversaw the torture and execution of several female prisoners accused of sorcery.

Later, when the fervor over witches had had died down in England (though beginning to spike in the Colonies), James claimed to have never been a proponent of the witchcraft crusade in his country, an outright lie perhaps indicative of the guilt he may have felt for his own part in the mania.

Over the next two years James published two political manifestos, *The True Law of Free Monarchies* and *Basilikon Doron*, tracts in which he proclaimed to be chosen by God for kingship. Under this delusion of divine leadership, James sought to stamp out public vices for which he was not favorably disposed. He cracked down famously on alcohol, gambling, prostitution, and most zealously of all, nicotine.

Was He or Wasn't He?

One of the great mysteries regarding the life of King James concerns his sexuality. During the era, rumors swirled that the King was gay and many of his past male "courtiers" and "favourites" were in fact his lovers. James was rarely seen in the company of women (helping to fuel the rumors) and so a hasty marriage was arranged with Anne of Denmark, who had just turned 14. Though the couple produced seven offspring, it is thought that James lead a dual life throughout most of his reign.

King James' first alleged lover was his 37 year old cousin, Esmé Stewart, whom the 13 year old James was often seen kissing openly in public. The Church of Scotland warned James' forebears that Stewart was attempting to seduce the young man, which lead to Esmé being banished to France and ordered to never see James again. (The two men, however, kept up a secret correspondence for the next several years.)

Next on the list was the First Earl of Somerset, Robert Carr. The 41 year old King took a great liking to the 17 year old Earl, and it was considered common knowledge at the time that the two were involved in a sexual relationship. One letter written by James and sent to the young Carr complained about the Earl's "withdrawing yourself from lying in my chamber, notwithstanding my many hundred times earnest soliciting you to the contrary." Another letter from around the same time has Carr praising the size of the King's member.

Their relationship ended badly amidst the backdrop of a murder scandal and Carr's attempted blackmail of King James over their "sodomous relayshions." Carr outlived James by twenty years, and would often speak of their affair to anyone who would listen.

Unlike his semi-secret relationship with Robert Carr, James took every opportunity he could to publicly proclaim his love for George Villiers, Duke of Buckingham. The two regularly sent each other love letters explicitly recounting their past sexual liaisons and as contemporary poet Théophile de Viau wrote: "it is well known that the king of England f**ks the Duke of Buckingham." A 2005 restoration of Apethorpe Hall unearthed a hidden passage that connected James and Villiers' bedchambers.

Given the overwhelming amount of evidence available, most modern historians will at least concede that King James was likely bisexual- an irony sometimes lost on the throngs of people who use his version of the Bible to condemn the very practice that he himself may have been a practitioner of.

THE CRACKDOWN ON TOBACCO

It is not known why King James developed such an ingrained hatred of what he termed "the vile, stinking weed." but many modern scholars believe that it stemmed from his dislike of Sir Walter Raleigh.

There had long been a rivalry between the two, Raleigh having been a favorite of Queen Elizabeth and thus seen as a threat by the increasingly paranoid James. King James also suspected Raleigh to be behind many of the slanderous rumors concerning his sexuality (see sidebar). James took every opportunity to ridicule Raleigh's tobacco habit, even famously remarking that "a tobacco pipe is characterized by having a flame on one end and a fool at t'other."

Upon James' ascension to England's throne, one of his first official acts was to arrest Raleigh for treason, claiming that he was behind a recent assassination attempt on James' life. The charges were mostly groundless, which is perhaps why James spared Raleigh the death sentence despite a guilty verdict against him.

Raleigh remained imprisoned in the Tower of London for another 13 years before being released to find the fabled Lost City of Gold. During his expedition, Raleigh's men were attacked by Spanish villagers and proceeded to massacre their encampment. (Raleigh's own son perished in the melee). As punishment, the King of Spain demanded that King James reinstate Raleigh's death sentence- a request that James was only too happy to grant.

While preparing to accept the crown of England, James wrote *A Counterblaste to Tobacco*, the first significant treatise against the "vile sin" of tobacco taking. It was published anonymously in 1604, perhaps realizing that his unpopular views could hurt his reputation among his subjects. It would be another twelve years before he would admit to authoring the tract. (It is rumored that James himself sent the work to all 7,000 of England's tobacconists with the exhortation to display it in plain view of all customers).

His *Counterblaste* having failed to quell the growing number of smokers as he had hoped, James next arranged the first public debate against tobacco, held at Oxford University. He displayed the blackened brains and organs that he claimed were taken from the bodies of dead smokers (though in all likelihood the organs were preserved in a particular state of decay that made them appear darker than normal.) This spectacle also failed to end smoking in England, so James sought other means to discourage the "epidemik."

The first thing he did was to ban the growing of tobacco within England. By monopolizing the trade, he also intended to limit the amount being grown in the Colonies and to (naturally) maximize his own revenue. This crackdown failed so spectacularly that he, with great fury, raised the import duty on tobacco from 2 pence per pound to an astounding 6 shilling & 8 pence. This startling increase in taxes accomplished nothing except to make smuggling more rampant. In retaliation, James increased the tax again 40-fold and made tobacco smuggling a

Above: *Sir Walter Raleigh, arch-nemesis of King James I.*

Below: *The Jamestown Colony of Virginia was heavily dependent on the tobacco crops that were constantly threatened by the King's incessant taxation.*

Right: *First printing of the King James Bible.*

Left: *King James, aged 22.*

crime punishable by death. This last ditch effort to regulate the plant was no more successful than his earlier attempts, and by 1608 the King had to admit that he had been defeated.

Realizing that he would never be able to end tobacco use, James came to terms with the practice and in a stunning reversal of previous policy decreased the tax on tobacco to 1 shilling per pound, which was half the amount that was in place when he first took office. This was beneficial not only to British tobacco users, but to the American colony that bared James' name. Tobacco growth and export continued to swell for the next five years until a new problem arose.

By concentrating on tobacco plants, both the American colonists and the British farmers had neglected to grow essential food crops which meant that there was a shortage in both countries. To attempt to discourage tobacco growth in England, King James barred anyone from planting it without a letter patent (which entitled the government to half of the farmer's profits).

In an almost exact replay of the previous decade's events, smuggling increased and James retaliated by raising the tax yet again. In 1620, he enacted the Stamp Law which required all tobacco sold to England to bear a government stamp (with the cost of the stamp falling on the shipper, not the buyer). This outraged the Virginia colonists, who in a foreshadowing of the Revolutionary War still 150 years away, refused the taxation and threatened to end shipments to England.

When news of the rebellion reached England, tobacco users began to furiously horde their supply in anticipation of the possible cutoff in shipments. The people appealed to Parliament, who in turn took James to task for his continuous "meddling" in what had heretofore proven to be such a profitable trade. The House of Commons then passed a series of reforms that protected the Colonists from undue taxation and, most importantly, sent them extra supplies to help them along in their endeavor.

This assistance lead to a renewed quality of tobacco crop, and within a few years the Virginia tobacco was outselling, at a premium, the crop being imported from all other countries (including Spain, who until recently had been regarded as the premiere source of fine tobacco.)

Of Medicine and Nicotine

King James hatred of tobacco was especially ironic considering that his grandmother, the Queen of France Catherine de Medici, helped to popularize tobacco use through the form of snuff taking.

French Ambassador to Portugal Jean Nicot was given the gift of several tobacco plants, which he mistook for medicine. After crumbling one of the leaves into dust and wiping some of the powder onto his nose and forehead, he found himself relieved of a nagging headache that had been plaguing him for days.

Knowing that the queen likewise suffered from persistent migraines, Nicot sent a box of the snuff to de Medici, who was astounded to find that it made her headaches vanish. Over the next several decades, the practice of snuffing would become a favored activity by both the aristocracy and the common people before gradually being supplanted by tobacco smoking.

JEAN NICOT (LEFT) AND QUEEN OF FRANCE CATHERINE DE MEDICI (BELOW)

Nicot, though not the first European to import tobacco, was nevertheless given the honor of having both the plant genus *Nicotiana* and tobacco's active ingredient, nicotine, named after him. de Medici later died in comparative obscurity from a lung infection, a condition that many historians have erroneously blamed on her prodigious snuff use.

James was quite proud that his ragged group of American upstarts were able to finally best the hated Spain. In 1624, he created the Royal Tobacco Monopoly which decreed that the only tobacco that was allowed to be imported into England came from the Jamestown Colony.

While this ensured that America would soon become a burgeoning trade center in its own right, the Monopoly banned British farmers from growing any more tobacco whatsoever. Bloody riots ensued, which concerned the King very little given that he was virtually on his deathbed. After his death the following year, most of the more restrictive clauses of the Tobacco Monopoly Act were lifted in order to promote peace within the kingdom.

So was King James a brilliant visionary, 400 years ahead of his time? Or was he, as one of his detractors called him, a "contemptible, foolish tyrant?" Maybe Sir Anthony Weldon put it best when he described King James as the "wisest fool in Christendom."

Regardless, people are still talking about him four centuries after his death, which surely would have pleased him to no end.

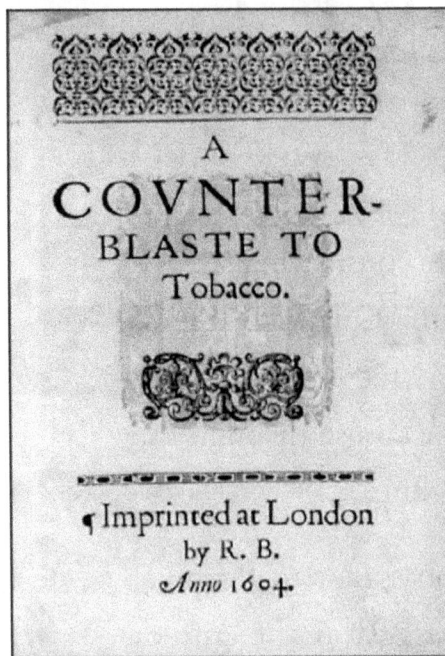

STE

A
COVNTER-
BLASTE TO
Tobacco.

¶ Imprinted at London
by R. B.
Anno 1604.

TITLE PAGE TO THE ORIGINAL 1604 EDITION (LEFT) AND A 1672 REPRINT (BOTTOM)

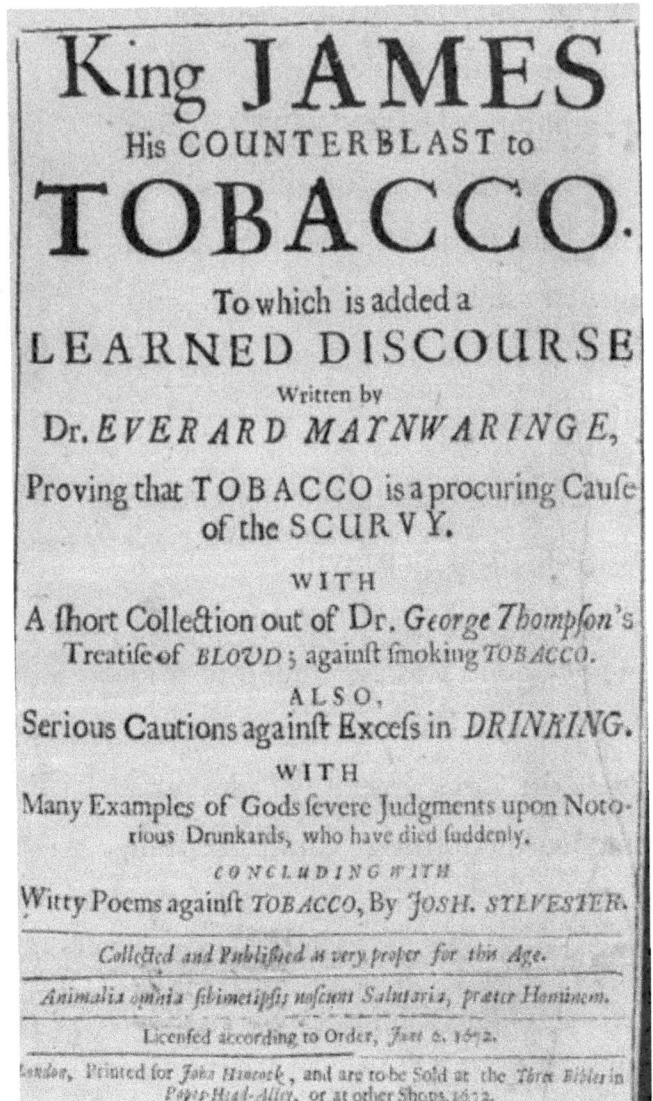

King JAMES
His COUNTERBLAST to
TOBACCO.
To which is added a
LEARNED DISCOURSE
Written by
Dr. *EVERARD MAYNWARINGE*,
Proving that TOBACCO is a procuring Cause
of the SCURVY.

WITH
A short Collection out of Dr. *George Thompson's*
Treatise of BLOVD; against smoking TOBACCO.

ALSO,
Serious Cautions against Excess in DRINKING.

WITH
Many Examples of Gods severe Judgments upon Notorious Drunkards, who have died suddenly.

CONCLUDING WITH
Witty Poems against TOBACCO, By *JOSH. SYLVESTER.*

Collected and Published as very proper for this Age.

Animalia omnia sibimetipsis nosciunt Salutaria, præter Hominem.

Licensed according to Order, *June* 6. 1672.

London, Printed for *John Hancock*, and are to be Sold at the *Three Bibles* in
Popes-Head-Alley, or at other Shops, 1672.

A Counterblaste To

Tobacco

A Complete Paraphrasis of the Original King James Text (In Modern English) as Translated by The Snuff Taker's Ephemeris

Introduction.

Dear Countrymen,

Just as every human, no matter how healthy, is subject to at least the occasional illness; there is no healthy government that is not naturally inclined to some corruption.

Therefore, it is no wonder that though we are a peace-loving and wealthy nation, reverently obedient to our Prince, we are often quick to rebel over the slightest offense. Our valor and victories displayed in wars abroad have bid us a long standing peace. Our peace has bred wealth, and our wealth has bred sluggishness.

This general malaise has brought forth idle comfort and soft delicacies- the first seeds of rebellion against all great Monarchies. Our clergy have become negligent and lazy. Our gentry and our noblemen have become errant and dependent upon their creature comforts. Our lawyers are covetous. Our commoners more adventurous and curious and, in general, everyone seems more inclined to look out for himself rather than for their mother, the Commonwealth.

As a remedy, it is the King's duty to purge the country of its diseases with a mild (but fair) government. It is his duty to quell the rebellions of commoners and to make us ashamed of our own vices. May he wake the clergy up with his strong admonitions and make them become more diligent. By quick trial and severe punishment may he reform the lying, covetous lawyers. And as a sterling example of his own character and by execution of due law, may he reform the populace and abolish these abuses.

There are always such abuses in any population. Often they are too vast a problem for the law to deal with, yet too minor an offense for the King to become involved. But they are all crimes, no matter how small. And in any country, not only the King- but anyone on his staff- should be able to recognize these errors and persuade the populace to mend their errant behavior.

And in my opinion, there can not be a more vile, base corruption in a country than the use of tobacco. This abuse in our own country has lead me to write the following little pamphlet. If anyone thinks it is a light argument, then so be it; but if my argument proves to be true, this is all that I seek. If it persuades one to change his outlook, then it is all that I can wish for (and more than I can expect.)

My only care, dear countrymen, is that you can understand the sincerity of my meaning even in this small tract. I will never cease to toil for your wealth and prosperity.

So that the many abuses of this vile custom of tobacco-taking can be better understood, consider the manner in which it was first introduced into this country. Just as all virtuous customs are brought in by godly and respectable authorities, all bad habits are introduced by corrupt and savage people under the guise of novelty. This was how tobacco was brought to England.

Tobacco grows wild nearly anywhere, and is called a variety of names by different cultures. The barbaric Indians of America use tobacco as a preservative and as an antidote against the pox- a filthy disease, which we all know these savages are prone to- brought on by their unsanitary living conditions and the intemperate heat of North America.

And so it was that these barbarians brought forth venereal disease to civilized people, and along with it the filthy antidote that they called tobacco. This stinking smoke they *still* use to treat Syphilis, pitting one poison against another.

And now good countrymen, I ask: what would make us imitate the beastly manners of such a wild, godless and slavish people- *especially* in such a vile and stinking custom? Shall we cease to imitate our Christian neighbors in France and instead act like Spaniards, to whom these Indians are enslaved to? This heathen, human refuse? Why don't we walk around naked like they do? Or prefer glass and feathers over gold and silver or deny God and worship Satan as they do?

This generation doesn't quite remember the first introduction of tobacco into England, but it wasn't brought here by the King or his physician. Our first conquest into America brought back three savages, who brought with them this custom. The pity of it all is that though the three men eventually died, their vile custom lived on.

It seems a miracle to me that so filthy a practice, brought here by a race of people so despised, would be so readily adopted by the population. If the earliest European tobacco users had realized what disease the plant was originally used to treat, they would have been loath to adopt the custom. For an antidote to work, there must first be a poison for it to fight.

But regardless, this was how tobacco entered England. Next, we shall examine whether tobacco has any merit or if the loathsome, hurtful use of this stinking antidote is but a baseless and foolish vice.

Below: "The Syphilitic Man." *The Italians called it "The Frenchman's Disease" while the French referred to it as "The Italian Sickness." The later, more prevalent view held that Columbus brought it back from the American Indians. In all likelihood, it was Columbus's crew that introduced the disease to the Americas, along with measles, smallpox, influenza, and bubonic plague (among others).* **Right, Following Pages:** *Anonymous 1612 woodcutting, often included with later printings of* Counterblaste.

Best baccy Ho ! Come buy my ware,
Each one of you must have his share.

I smoke too much, it makes me retch,
Ah look away now, I beseech !

II.

I now beg you to consider first the spurious grounds on which you condone your tobacco use and secondly, the sins towards God and foolishness towards man that you display by using it. Of these deceitful grounds that you have deluded yourself into accepting, I shall address four.

First, it is a common belief that since a man's brain is cold and wet, it needs to be balanced with something hot and dry (like tobacco smoke). Of this theory, both the assumption and proposition are both false, as is the conclusion. For man is comprised of four complexions (themselves derived from the four elements) and these disparate complexions form a uniquely balanced constitution.

The introduction therefore of any contrary substance to one of the complexities interrupts their function, thereby causing the entire body to become sick. A man wouldn't eat lead to cool his hot liver, nor would he place a heavy stone over his heart to quiet the palpitations. So should you not attempt to dry out the naturally moist brain matter, lest you go mad by attempting to maintain some sort of unobtainable "balance."

I do not deny that in certain situations, an infirmity may arise due to an imbalance in the complexions, and in these cases it may be useful to aid mother nature's path to recovery with a remedy administered by a trained physician. But these cures ought not to be used unless there is a genuine sickness, and the general use of tobacco is contrary to this practice.

Next, I believe that in addition to the hot and dry qualities of tobacco smoke, there exists a certain poisonous fume that joins with the heat and gives off a hateful stench which serves to warn us of its harmful

DIAGRAM SHOWING THE "FOUR HUMOURS", A DISCREDITED MEDICAL THEORY THAT KING JAMES RELIED UPON HEAVILY FOR HIS "SCIENTIFIC" HYPOTHESIS.

nature. Our nose acts as a conduit to the brain, and it registers whether a substance is helpful or harmful to our body based on the scent.

It is also a fact that the smoke does not possess a drying quality to it. No further evidence of this is needed other than that it is *smoke*, and all smoke and vapor is inherently humid. Rain drops, for example, are made of nothing more than the air and vapors on earth being sucked up by the sun and released as snow, dew, frost and hail. In contrast, rain clouds often evaporate and transform into blustering winds.

The second argument (that smoke purges the sinuses of congestion) is false, as proven by my earlier description of how rain is formed. For even as the smoky vapors of earth are sucked up by the sun and turned into moist rain, so does the stinking smoke enter the cold, damp brain and drain out as excess mucous. You are no more purged of snot by smoking tobacco and coughing, than you would be healed of the colic by eating gassy foods and farting; nor would you be cured of kidney stones by ingesting all manner of meats and drinks that breed bladder gravel.

As for the two remaining arguments, let us first examine the theory that the people of this country would have never taken to tobacco had it not been good for them. For an answer to that age-old question of why people are easily drawn to such foolish novelties, I leave it to the discreet judgement of any reasonable person.

I need my baccy it does me good,
It calms the ague and clears the blood.

My nose is all blocked up, I fear,
It needs a dose of snuff to clear.

III.

Many times we've seen a man come back from another country wearing a new style of clothing, and the people here rush to imitate that style, lest they be thought of as behind the times. And so it spreads from hand to hand, till it is worn by everyone- not because there is any usefulness to it, but only because it is the fashion.

For such is the force of natural self-love and envy that is within us all that we cannot be content unless we imitate everything that everyone else does (like the apes do). For example, let a math professor point out a strange apparition in the sky and watch his students also witness the same phenomena (even if they don't see anything) lest they be thought stupid or hard of sight. The embracing of this foolish custom does nothing but lead to the type of widespread ignorance that I've already spoken of.

The other argument drawn from this erroneous belief is that many are cured of divers disease, therefore tobacco must be safe. This is absurd. When a man is at the height of his illness and then takes tobacco, and when his body begins to naturally cure itself, the patient exclaims that it must have been the *tobacco* that healed him! It is a known fact among physicians that by exercise and movement, the patient has strengthened his body and has naturally set it towards healing itself of divers disease.

For proof of the above example, I ask you: what foolish boy, what silly wench, what old doting wife, or what ignorant country clown doesn't have a "remedy" for such common maladies as the toothache, colic or divers disease? Every man you will ever meet will swear that either he or someone he knows has been cured by such a remedy. And yet, I hope that nobody is foolish enough to believe him.

So if a man happens to recover from such a disease, tobacco gets the praise. Yet if a man smokes himself to death with it (as many have done) than some other disease must be at fault. Old whores claim that their whoring is what keeps them healthy in old age; sex (they say) being a healthy pastime. But nevermind how many die of venereal disease in the prime of their life. And so do drunkards claim to prolong their lives with their swine's diet, conveniently forgetting the many that die at half their age drowning in drink.

And who's to say that by curing divers, tobacco doesn't cause some other sort of disease? Like all doctors can attest, there is no medicine available that isn't harmful to some part of the body. As the old saying goes, "that which is good for the head is bad for the neck and shoulders." Like an enemy that circles a fortress trying to find the weakest area to attack, so does disease scan the body for the weakest organ to infect.

The skilled doctor knows which cure to employ that will not only destroy the illness in the affected areas, but to do the least amount of damage to the unaffected areas. He will take into account the nature of the climate the patient resides in, or any other special

Both wine and beer my pleasure earn.
Tobacco too shall have its turn.

Forgive me, snuff's a purge I warrant,
This wind escapes me in a torrent.

circumstances that may hinder treatment, the position of the planets, the location of the moon, the season of the year, along with the age and condition of the patient. For one cure can never be used to treat all disease, though this miraculous omnipotence has been attributed to tobacco.

If you were to believe what users say, then tobacco cures all forms of discomfort in the head and stomach. In actuality, it causes unnaturally quick digestion which fills the bowels with waste matter.

They say that it cures the gout of the foot, as if by some miracle the smoke travels down to the little toe and works its magic. It cures malaria. It sobers a drunken man. It soothes hunger, yet at the same time stirs the appetite. If taken at bedtime, it helps one sleep soundly; yet if taken when tired, it awakens the senses and restores vitality. As for the curing of syphilis, it only works on Indians. Here in England, the tobacco is refined and will not cure anything other than clean, gentlemanly diseases.

Omnipotent power of tobacco! If this smoke could only chase out devils, it would be a precious relic both for the superstitious priests and the insolent Puritans. Supposing that there was benefit to smoking, should it be used to cure all disease? Should it be used by young, strong, able and healthy men? Just like any medicine, if abused and taken regularly, it makes a man lethargic and useless. Such abuse is rampant in this kingdom, to the point that a smoker is unable to do without tobacco the same way an alcoholic can't bear to go without drink. Their addiction has weakened them in such a way that they react to healthy food as if it were poison.

1626 WOODCUTTING DEPICTING A MAN SMOKING A PIPE AT THE DINNER TABLE, MUCH TO THE CHAGRIN OF HIS DISAPPROVING FAMILY.

IV.

I trust that I have answered the most principle arguments that are used in defense of this vile custom. It serves solely to inform you of the sins and vanities you commit while abusing this plant. Are you not guilty of sinful, shameful lust (lust being a product of mind *or* body)? Though you are in perfect health, you cannot be merry at a party or randy at the brothel unless you have tobacco to prime you for these recreations, lusting after it as the Israelites lusted for quail in the wilderness.

Secondly, as you use (or rather, *abuse*) it, tobacco falls under the category of drunkenness, which is the root of all sins. For as the only delight that a drunkard gets from wine is the strength of the buzz that it gives him, an alcoholic doesn't care for weak, sweet drinks. Are not the strength and the smoke the only qualities of tobacco that a user finds so delectable? And as no man likes a strong, heady drink the first day (he must become accustomed to it bit by bit), is it not the same for a smoker?

Thirdly, is it not the greatest sin of all that you people of this Kingdom, created and ordained by God to give honor and safety to your king and country, fail on both counts? By this continuous vile behavior you're not even able to walk or ride a short distance, but must have someone else bring you a burning coal from the next poorhouse to light your tobacco!

A soldier can not be thought fit for battle unless he is able to go long periods without food, drink or sleep; but most importantly, he must be able to do without tobacco. Throughout the history of wars and battles fought for this country, there was no mention of tobacco. But if we were to go to war right now and our regiment staged an ambush against the enemy, I'm sure that there would be a soldier that stayed behind during the attack so that he could puff away leisurely on tobacco. I would never be sorry for the horrible fate that may befall him.

To make a custom out of anything that renders one useless is harmful to the people of any land. Such excess brought forth the fall of first the Persian and then the Roman empires. And this very custom of tobacco use has been found to be so debilitating that even the Indians themselves refuse to purchase a slave that uses great quantities of tobacco.

The people of this land make themselves poor through their addiction, some of them spending three or four hundred pounds a year on this precious stink. I'm sure this money could be put to far better use. I have never heard of so many single smoke buyers in any given land.

I read of a courtier who was taking bribes from lobbyists in order to intercede to the emperor (himself unaware of such extortion) on their behalf. He was deservedly choked to death with tobacco smoke, *fumo pereat, qui fumum vendidit.* (He who sells the smoke, dies by the smoke).

And as for the vanity that comes along with tobacco use, is it not a great display of gluttony and un-cleanliness that men

are not ashamed to sit at the dinner table (a place of modesty, hygiene and respect) smoking tobacco pipes and puffing the filthy, stinky smoke and exhaling it towards the dishes and infecting the air while the other guests are still eating their dinner? Surely it would be more appropriate to smoke in the kitchen rather than the dining chamber, but even still this smoke travels into the lungs of other men and infects them with the same kind of oily soot that has been found in dead smokers during autopsy.

And it's not just dinner that is ruined by smokers. The public use of tobacco is now so prevalent that even sound, intelligent men have started to smoke- partly so that they won't seem behind the times and partly so that it doesn't bother them as much. (Remember the man who hated garlic? He ate it anyway because everyone at his dinner party was consuming it and the stench only became bearable after he himself ate some.)

And is it not a great vanity that a man can't heartily welcome his friend over to his home unless he has a supply of tobacco on hand? No, it has become an example of good hosting manners. And a man that refuses the pipe is deemed peevish and not thought to be good company. Yea, the hostess can not be considered polite unless she greets her guests with a pipe of tobacco.

But this is not only a great vanity, but an affront to God. For a man's sweet breath is one of God's great gifts, and to corrupt it with stinking smoke is a crime against nature. Moreover, a man will corrupt his wife to smoke lest she resolves to live her life in a perpetual stinking torment. It is an iniquity against humanity.

Have you no reason then to be ashamed and forego this filthy novelty? In your abuse you sin against God, harming both your body and your belongings, taking the marks of vanity upon you. Your habit makes you a spectacle to other nations and a contemptible scorn to all who immigrate here.

Tobacco: a custom loathsome to the eye, hateful to the nose, harmful to the brain, dangerous to the lungs; its black, stinking smoke most closely resembling that of the horrible Stygian fumes from the bottomless pit.

STE

www.snuscentral.com

www.facebook.com/snuscentral

WARNING: Smokeless tobacco is addictive.

Snuff movies

Bonnie Scotland

1935
Starring Stan Laurel & Oliver Hardy
Directed by James Horne

Bonnie Scotland is a lackluster entry in the long-running series of films that comedy duo Laurel and Hardy made between 1921 and 1951.

The threadbare plot centers around Laurel and Hardy breaking jail and sailing to Scotland to in order to collect an inheritance from Laurel's grandfather. The inheritance turns out to be nothing more than a snuffbox and a broken set of bagpipes. From there, the two enlist in the army and end up stationed in India, spending the rest of the movie running around kicking over beehives. (Seriously).

The film was doomed from the start. Originally running almost 80 minutes, the studio chopped it down to a 60 minute run time in order to make it somewhat watchable. Unfortunately, this hack job made the movie completely incomprehensible, and it was quickly reissued at 70 minutes. Eventually, the entire 80 minute opus was re-released in the USA under the title *Heroes of the Regiment.*

The one good bit in the entire film happened to be the infamous snuffbox scene, in which the two bumbling clods attempt to hone the fine art of snuffing. (Unsurprisingly, they fail miserably.) Presented here for your perusal is a still-by-still storyboard of the entire sequence.

(1) Stan Laurel fiddles about with his snuffbox, takes a pinch...

(2) ... and sticks it under his tongue, Norwegian style.

(3) "That's not how you use that stuff!" Hardy takes an elegant pinch...

(4) ... shakes off the excess...

(5) ...takes a nice jolt into his right nostril...

(6) ... then the left...

(7) ... shakes off the crumbs...

(8) "There, now you try."

(9) ... takes a pinch...

(10) ... takes a sniff...

(11) "Ahhhhhhh.....

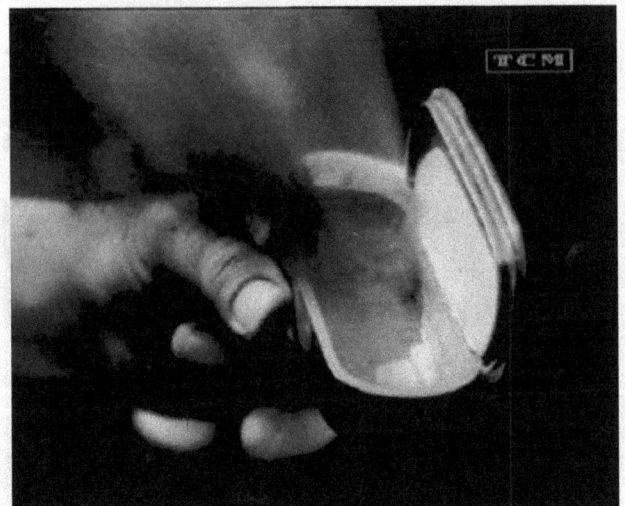
(12) ... CHOO!!!!"

(13) The snuff flies into Hardy's face, causing him to reel back...

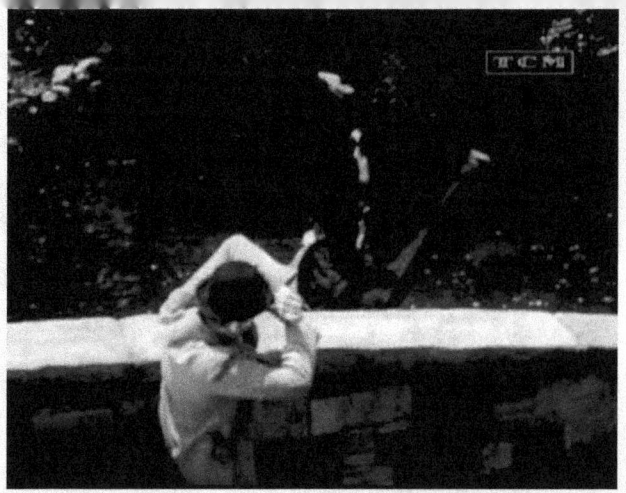
(14) ... and fall off the bridge.

(15) While underwater, he sneezes so violently...

(16) ... That he expels all the water from the pond.

(17) "Hey, lardass..."

(18) "...you suck at planking!"

STE

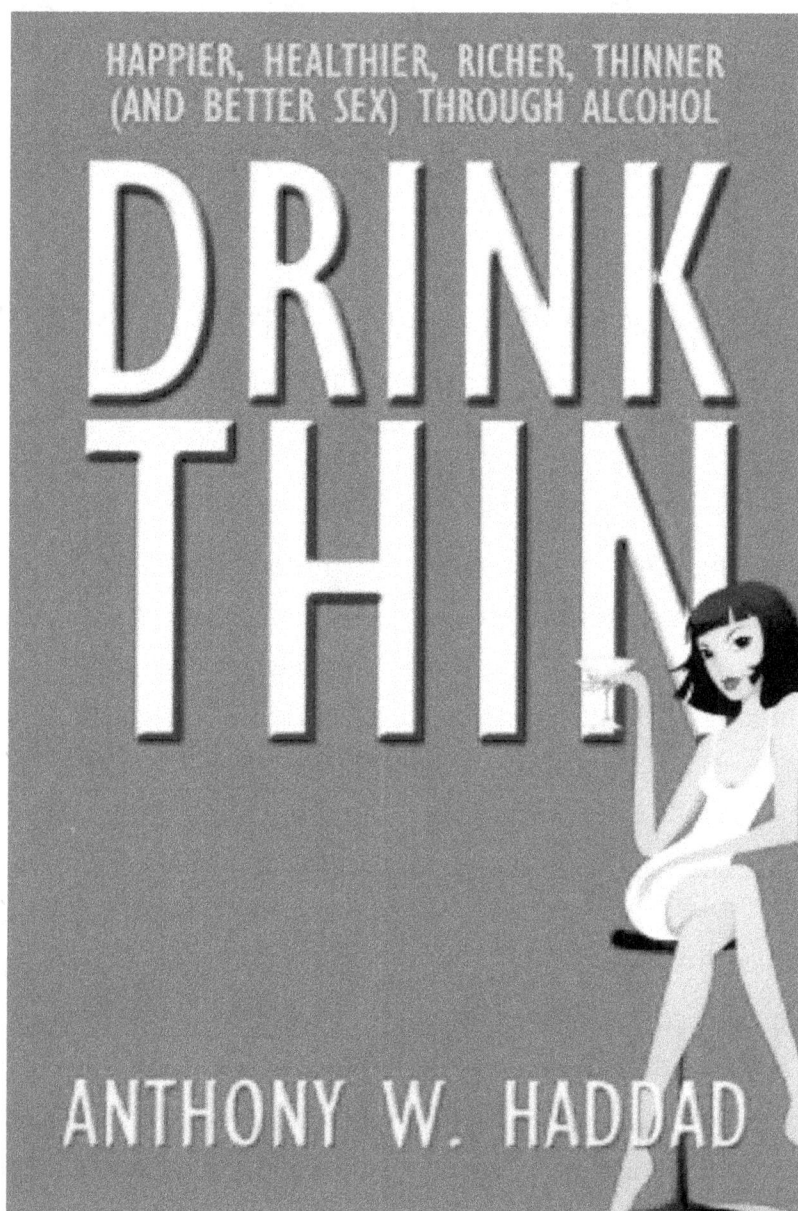

Quackery!

The Hindoo Tobacco Habit Cure

Roberta Bivins, in her excellent *Alternative Medicine: A History*, says of The Hindoo Tobacco Cure that "the remedy was as Indian as Indiana." This was not an exaggeration- the tiny Milford, Indiana firm Milford Drug Company (not to be confused with any of the other dozens of similarly named Milford Drug companies active at the same time) had long been turning out "natural" medicines for half a century.

Beginning in the 1850's, MDC started turning out patent elixirs (popularly referred to as "snake oil" by the more skeptical consumers of the day) and like most tonics and "revitalizers" of the era were comprised mainly of alcohol and opiate extract. One such Milford product, "Poppy Milk", could quite literally be called a morphine milkshake, It combined the relatively new phenomena of evaporated milk with the time-honored relief of opium. One ad even suggested giving Poppy Milk to fidgety children would help control their "outbursts" (nowadays we just give them ritalin and send them to school).

By the late 1890s the danger of opium-derived products was becoming common knowledge and Milford Drug Company decided to switch tactics. Their new "Hindoo Tobacco Cure" was a powdered dose (similar to a Goody or BC headache powder) that was comprised of "safe, all natural roots and herbs" like cocaine and hemlock. MDC even cheekily offered "$5,000 to anyone who can show that we use opium, morphine, or any other harmful drugs in this remedy" when a decade earlier it had flooded the market with products comprised of such ingredients.

Nevertheless, the Hindoo Cure disappeared with most other drugs of the era after the federal crackdown that took place in the early 20th century. The small wooden box that it came in is highly collectible and the few examples that reach the market today command top dollar at auction.

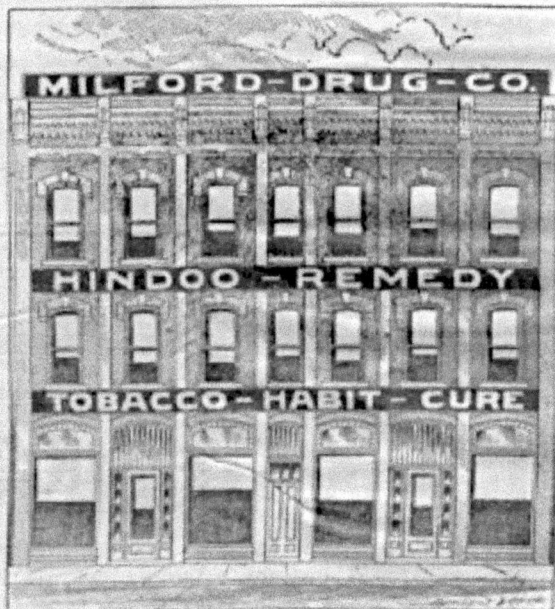

www.snuscentral.com   www.facebook.com/snuscentral

BLACKGUARD OF THE MONTH

Chuck Hamsher, Coalition For A Tobacco-Free West Virginia

Chuck Hamsher, an "artist", antique dealer and interior decorator from Charleston, WV knows what's best for you and your family. As an advocacy director for the American Heart Association and as a lobbyist for Tobacco Free West Virginia, he's attempting to introduce a bill that will raise the tax on smokeless tobacco from 7 percent of the wholesale price to 55 percent. The bill also calls for a 1.00 increase on the cigarette tax, up from .55.

But like all liberals that try and force their opinions on the public through increased legislation, Hamsher refuses to call a spade a spade. "It's not a tax," he claims. "It's a public health measure. Tobacco is a plague among the land." (Note to our readers: if you want to see a *real* plague, check out the gallery of abstract paintings featured on Hamsher's website.)

"The tobacco tax [*hey, I thought it was a public health measure*] is one of the proven strategies to reduce usage," he said with a straight face, before adding that "it prevents kids from picking it up." Come again? How is raising the price on a product going to prevent kids from trying it, being that they can't purchase it in the first place? That's as stupid as raising the federal income tax in order to dissuade illegal aliens from crossing our borders.

He went on to say that "it encourages adults to quit and it equalizes the playing field as well. Smokers will begin paying their fair share to the state." Wait a minute- if the tax forces all the tobacco users to give up their habit- how is the state going to get its "fair share"? I guess

Chuck Hamsher, in a candidly pretentious self-shot photomosaic .

they'll have to start taxing the hell out of the only other significant source of revenue in West Virginia- the coal industry. Wait... he wants to increase the coal taxes too? Geez, this guy must think he lives in Oregon.

West Virginian snuffers shouldn't worry too much, though. This proposal was killed last year and it hasn't garnered much support this year either. Said republican delegate Jonathon Miller: "Trying to stop people from using tobacco is not the purpose of government taxing its citizens. Government taxes people to pay for government services, not to coerce them to engage or not to engage in a particular activity. It is morally wrong for the government to use the force of taxation to manipulate people's behavior."

STE

INDIAN SNUFF CULTURE

By Nigel McCarren

When Indian snuff, carried on the currents of the internet, arrived on western shores we became aware of a whole new snuff tradition that had been hitherto unknown outside of the sub-continent. Those first imports tended to be hyper fine, deeply perfumed and ferociously strong and were the province of the seasoned user for whom a sneeze was unknown and high dried or scotch snuffs the standard pinch.

That is not to say the new products were in any way unrefined, but they carried a certain exclusivity with them due to their punching power. Not content with a niche market serving scotch, toast and chili insufflators, the Indians started to make excellent Western-style snuffs, often as contract brands for the online retailers. It was this phase of the entry into our domestic markets that probably secured their future. Over the last four or five years they have become part of the snuff institution and we are now seeing other exciting companies join the market.

One of those is the 6 Photo Snuff Company. In January 2012 I interviewed the owner, Mr Vikas Grover, in order to get a general sense of the Indian snuff culture and its history. "According to the GATS India survey for 2009-10," explained Vikas, "there are 206 million users of smokeless tobacco in India. Smokeless tobacco products include Khaini (snus), chewing tobacco (gutkha, panmasala and betel quid with tobacco) and dentifrice tobacco products like gul, gudaku, mishri and cream snuff. The share of these dentifrice products is 5% of the total smokeless tobacco use. Gutka, chewing tobacco and khaini comprise about 75% of the total use.

Snuff is more commonly used by females as a dentifrice and they tend to be from rural or manual labouring sections of the populace. There are around 111 million smokers in India - with cigarettes in the city and traditional 'biris' in country areas."

206 million! Roughly four times the population of the United Kingdom and a large chunk of the US - all using smokeless tobacco products. Can 206 million Indian people be wrong? Maybe someone should point our politicians and health fascists East and whisper 'Go figure' in their ears. With smokeless tobacco being used on a two to one ratio, India could be the population for scientific study to finally establish the facts about smokeless tobacco use. If only the political will existed.

Supplying this amount of people with snuff is clearly a mammoth task and India has around one hundred different snuff companies. In comparison, the UK has half a dozen or so manufacturers.

Variation in snuff production is usually limited by region. "There are basically 5-6 towns in India where almost all of those production units are located, as well as some scattered units. All the snuff units in one centre produce similar types of snuff in similar looking packaging which is unique to that centre. Whilst there may be a subtle difference in flavoring, the look and feel of the snuff is the same.

The big snuff producing centres of India are:

Giddarbaha - The home of 6 Photo snuff in the north and famous for its black, perfumed snuff.

Sihor - In Gujarat; known for its yellow-colored, perfumed varieties as well as unflavored snuffs.

Beawar - In Rajasthan in the west, specializing in red, perfumed snuffs.

Chennai (formerly known as Madras)- Produces mainly unflavored, traditional varieties.

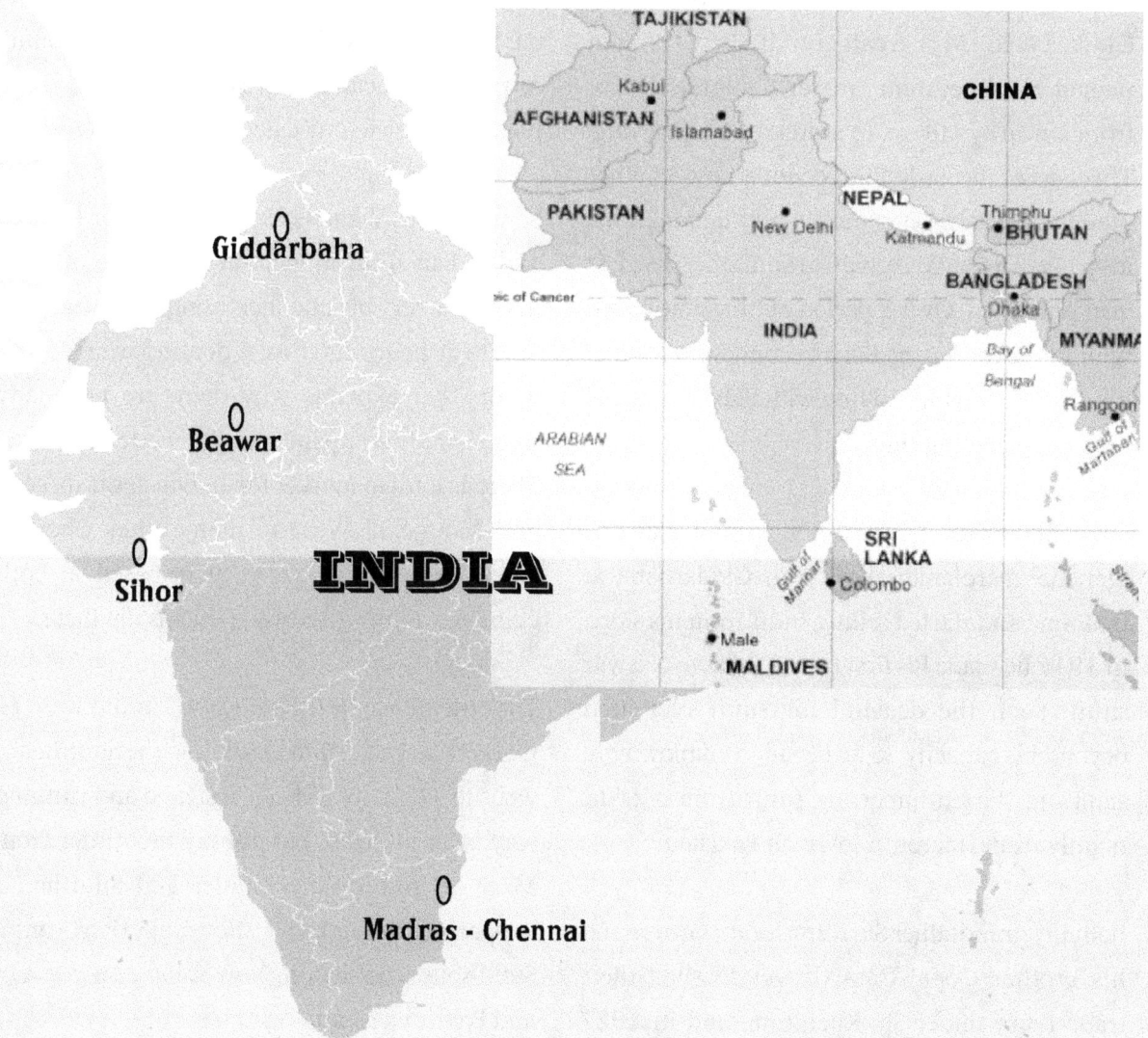

It is clear that there is a fantastic diversity of products available and, quite honestly, as a life-long snuff user I get light-headed at the prospect. Visions of back-packing in India, snuff box in hand, are hard to shake - any retailers reading this please take note.

Vikas, who lives in Giddarbaha, shared some background on the town. "Giddarbaha is a small town in Eastern Punjab- a state in northern India with a population of around 40,000. It is famous for two reasons: its unique black snuff, and the best Punjabi singer in India, Gurdas Mann.

There is a story behind the evolution of snuff in Giddarbaha. My great-grandfather, a man named Sh. Kheturam Grover, emigrated here from a nearby village, in search of better living. This was in the early 20th century, and another man named Baba Gangaram, a very famous saint, also lived here. My great-grandfather used to visit him often. Over a period of time, impressed with his devotion, the Baba become very fond of his disciple and blessed him with Baba's personal recipe for making snuff.

Sh. Kheturam owned a small kirana (general merchandise) shop in Giddarbaha at that time and started selling snuff from his store. In 1917 he made his first brand, 5 Photo Naswar snuff. Soon the demand for snuff increased beyond his capacity, so he began to employ more staff and started importing snuff from outside, mainly from Hazron, a town in Pakistan.

Both my grandfather Sh. Munshiram Grover and his brother Gopal Dass Grover learned their trade there under Sh. Kheturam, and in 1927 they launched their own brand; 6 Photo. The pictures on the label of 6 Photo snuff are of these two gentlemen. Many other former employees and relatives launched their own brands of snuff over time, and at present there are about 20-25 units making snuff in Giddarbaha."

Two of those units are headed by Vikas and his brother. "I finished college in 1993 and joined the family business. 6 Photo snuff is completely family owned - we are two brothers both heading separate units, making 6 Photo snuff with demarcated territories."

What of their closest competition, the 5 Photo company? "The 5 Photo unit reopened in 1995, but by that time we had gained sufficient ground. At present we can safely say that 6 Photo is the market leader in our category."

So what does Vikas see in the future for 6 Photo and Indian snuff in general? "The sale of snuff in India is very big and increasing, in my opinion, due to it being used as a dentifrice more and more. That explains why there are not many Indian snuff companies in the western market. There is a huge market for Indian snuff in Tibet and Mongolia. We and many other Chennai based companies have dealers based in both countries. Snuff is mostly used nasally there.

The emergence of 6 Photo snuff in the western market can be attributed solely to the Snuffhouse website. I had my website designed and running way back in 2006, but got my first order from Mr.Snuff (the online retailer and Snuffhouse supporter shop) only after appearing on a Snuffhouse discussion. Now we are on German and Polish websites also."

A Photo is worth a thousand words

A dig through the Ephemeris archives reveals no less than thirty separate Indian smokeless tobacco products all containing the word "photo" in the name, ranging from the 19th century to the present. What's with all this fascination with photography?

Tom Klein from Kosmos Collectibles explains: "Literacy in India was something of a rarity during the British Occupation. Many residents were unable to read the printed labels, so producers and advertisers went to great lengths to make bright, easy to understand packaging for their products."

"For example, one company would come up with a snuff called Elephant. It would have a giant elephant on the label. Another company, perhaps trying to cash in on the success of Elephant snuff, would make their own Elephant snuff, but this time it would have *two* Elephants on the label and be called 'Two Elephant.' This would go on until you had 8 Elephant, 9 Elephant and so on. The customer needn't be literate to pick out his brand in the store- he just counted the number of elephants on the package!"

This same formula applies to the Photo snuffs. "'Photograph' brands were pretty common in India, not just on tobacco products," Klein said. "The label would have a large photographed portrait of a revered *sadhu* or other notable person, and it would have smaller copies of the same portrait on the sides. One would count the number of photos to guess the brand name."

What's the most extreme example of this photo-numeric brand naming that Klein has come across? "Without a doubt, it's a coffee can from around 1900. The name could be translated as *towers* or *pillars*, and the number was 48. So you have 48 identical towers printed around the circumference of the can and it's pretty much impossible to count them all without losing track."

"I have a mental image of a frustrated villager standing in the store all day trying to count up these thin little stick towers, and then going home and having his wife bawl him out because he picked up 47 Tower coffee instead of 48."

The reception has been great so far. "Our 6 Photo snuffs have been warmly received by Western customers and we're getting very good reviews about our snuffs on Snuffhouse.org. This has led to repeat orders from Mr.Snuff and Snuffstore Germany."

It is clear that 6 Photo is not resting on its laurels and the development of new lines is an important part of the business plan.

"We have developed three new brands for the western market: the Natural, Medicated No. 6 and Medicated No.66. All three are getting rave reviews on Snuffhouse.

Besides these three we market seven other brands. Cheeta white snuff is our most popular brand in the west. We expect our new medicated varieties to move great volumes as well."

One thing that I have always liked about Indian snuffs is the sensitive use of medicating ingredients. There is a slightly unusual reason for this, as Vikas explains:

"As compared to the English and German snuffs, Indian snuffs use less menthol and are high in nicotine content mainly because of its use as a dentifrice. A high menthol content could be very irritating on the gums."

India sounds like a snuff taker's paradise, so I was surprised to find that it is so massively taxed. "In India, snuff is highly levied at 80% excise duty and 20%-40% sales tax, depending upon the state, along with many other various small taxes. The competition among the factories of a region is very fierce and business is highly competitive and secretive.

There is very little scope for any experimentation with new flavors or packaging in the Indian market. Any changes lead to rejection from the customer. Indian snuff users are highly brand loyal, but price conscious too, and they expect quality consistency that doesn't break with tradition all at an affordable price."

As in other countries, snuff is competing in a market dominated by cigarettes. "Smoking cigarettes is very prevalent in urban areas but the use of smokeless tobacco products and biris is much higher in rural areas. Gutkha is sold throughout the country in high volumes. There is no awareness about snuff among the urbanized, wealthy literate people. It is a product used mainly by the labour workers and rural folk."

Clearly, Indian snuff has found a permanent place in the hearts and snuff boxes of Western users and our enjoyment of this most elegant of tobacco products can only be enhanced as a result.

STE

Nigel McCarren is the owner/operator of Snuffhouse.org, the best nasal snuff forum on the web, Reviews of the 6 Photo range of snuffs can be found there.

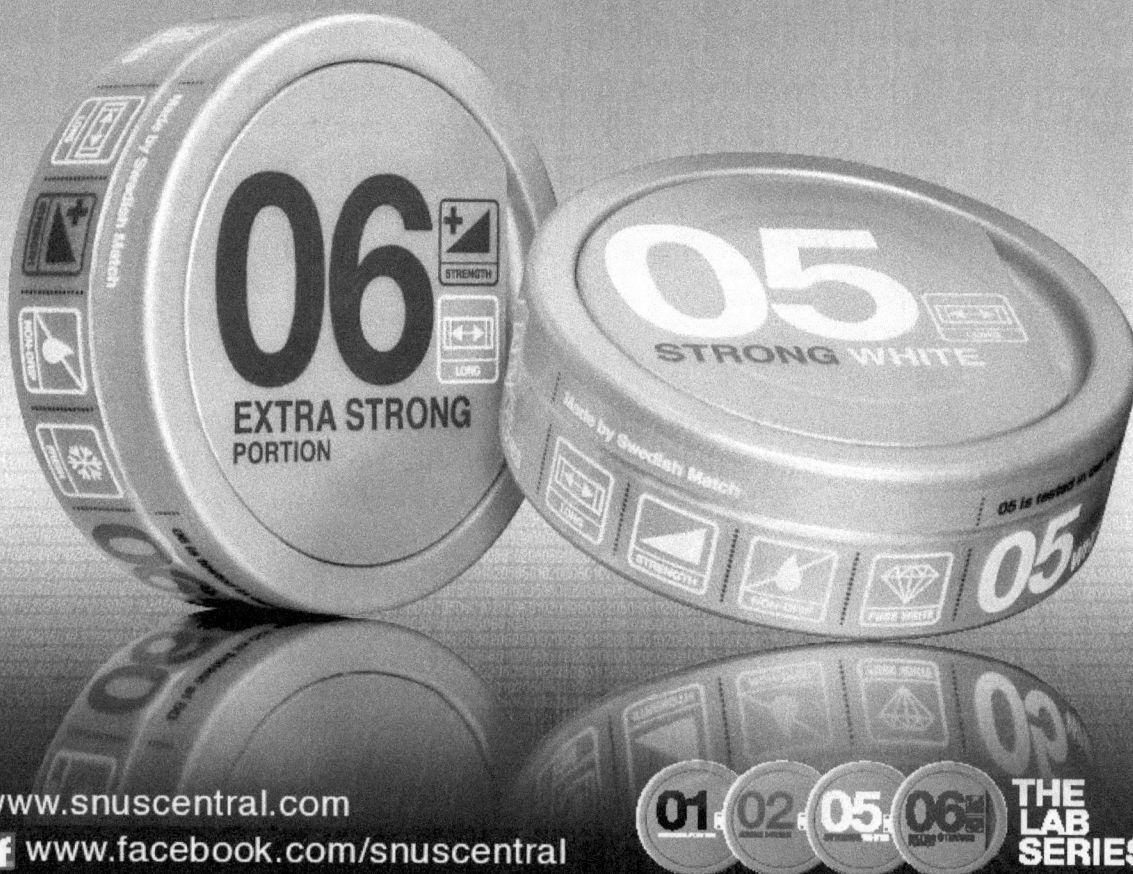

NEWS FROM THE LAB

06 EXTRA STRONG PORTION

05 STRONG WHITE

www.snuscentral.com
f www.facebook.com/snuscentral

01 02 05 06 THE LAB SERIES

Snus King:
Ljunglöf's Ettan
And the History of Swedish Snus

Part IV

Original text © 1999 by the Swedish Tobacco Museum

CHAPTER FOUR:

FROM THE MARSHES TO THE SWAMPS

KING KNUT

Jacob Fredrik Ljunglöf was well known for his snus and was a firm leader until his death in 1860. His son Knut took over production of the Ettan brand and made sure that the quality was still evident in every prillor.

Sweden was entering a new era and young Knut was a good symbol for this age. His father had sent him to Europe for a formal education. After studying business management in Bremen and language studies in Liverpool, Knut returned home ready to take over and run the factory.

Though he had grown up in the cramped, narrow confines of the old Queen Street factory in Stockholm, Knut returned home to find a sprawling, block-long business complex awaiting him. The spacious Ljunglöf home was impressive for its day, and was always open to visitors, who were welcome to walk right up to Ljunglöf's desk while he worked. (Knut, a firm but fair businessman, was not quite as open and inviting as his father).

SNUS KUNGEN: LJUNGLÖFS ETTAN OCH DET SVENSKA SNUSET IS CONSIDERED ONE OF THE BEST HISTORICAL ACCOUNT OF THE SWEDISH SNUS INDUSTRY. THE SWEDISH TEXT, UNFORTUNATELY, WAS NEVER TRANSLATED INTO ENGLISH.

THE EPHEMERIS PRESENTS A CHAPTER-BY-CHAPTER TRANSLATION OF THE ORIGINAL TEXT SO THAT THE STORY CAN BE SHARED WITH ALL.

Knut Fredrik Ljunglöf (1833 – 1920)

THE NEW SNUS FACTORY, 191 LUNTMAKARGATAN, STOCKHOLM.

The move to the new factory was necessary, for it was no longer feasible to trade snus for reindeer herds or furs. The economy was on the rise and people finally had cash to pay with, including the frontiersmen of Norrland- still Ljunglöf's largest market.

THE WEST SIDE OF THE BUILDING, WHERE DELIVERIES WERE LOADED OR DROPPED OFF.

THE MOVE TO THE SWAMP

Ljunglöf moved his home and business to Stockhom's Traskit (marshland) district in 1839. Shown here is the dining room foyer, nicknamed the "Red Room."

The Ettan factory was fully mechanized with the most state-of-the-art technology of the era. Though production was automated to some degree, each batch was personally monitored by the foreman. The men in this picture are shown checking the moisture content of the snus while it cooks in the steam chamber.

Shown here are workers from the factory's ground floor. This team handled all of the accounts payable work and oversaw the shipping department.

To The North

Population was sparse in the frozen hinterland to the north, but the forest and river country yielded great natural resources. Timber was needed for the burgeoning construction industry as well as for toothpicks, pencils, matchsticks, furniture and paper mills. The sawmills attracted a crop of new frontiersmen willing to work hard and better the lives of their families.

Though the work was brutal, the men enjoyed a camaraderie. Many nights were spent passing the bottle around and telling folktales by the campfire. But one thing that remained off-limits was one's personal snuffbox. Snus was hard to come by and fetched a hefty premium in the barren woods, and men were not eager to share the "brown gold."

Even lonelier were the smokestackers whose job it was to feed the charcoal stack round the clock. These men were slaves to a huge woodpile and their days were spent endlessly chopping timber and feeding it into giant ovens. These blackened, grizzled lumberjacks were admired by even the hardiest of workers. A sort of romanticized mythology grew around the smokestackers and their exploits were recounted in song and story.

The smokestackers weren't adverse to making up their own rhymes, either, as evidenced by this popular mid-19th century refrain:

> *Well the world is beautiful*
> *For those with cash*
> *That live in a nice stately house.*
>
> *But nothing free*
> *Was ever given to me*
> *So I guess I'll just buy a pinch of snus...*

THE RAILROADS

Knut wholeheartedly took advantage of another new technology booming in Sweden, railway transport. Freight trains transported Ettan all over the country, so that snus-happy Swedes everywhere were able to buy their favorite brand.

At that time, cattle were transported to the slaughterhouse in the same cars that housed dry goods. Before long, Knut was getting massive returns from vendors who refused delivery of his snus. Intrigued, Knut broke open a barrel of the rejected Ettan and was horrified to discover that it didn't taste like Ettan at all. The snus had a pungent, ammonia-like scent to it that reminded Ljunglöf of hospital disinfectant. (This only added insult to the injury; the superstitious Knut had a lifelong fear of hospitals and doctors).

The reason for the chemical taste was due to carbolic acid. The acid was sprayed into the railroad cars to halt the spread of hoof and mouth disease that came from the cattle being transported. The porous snus took on the lingering flavor of the chemicals in the air, which caused it to taste bad. Strict orders were issued from Ljunglöf headquarters: under no circumstance was Ettan to be loaded onto a cattle car ever again. With the kind of financial clout that Ljunglöf possessed, it was a safe bet that his warning was heeded.

Another problem that Knut faced was with snus packaging. Ettan was delivered in wooden kegs, called firkins, to be displayed at the store's counter and sold in bulk. (Some storekeeps were liberal with the product and charged a flat rate for a customer to dip his snuffbox into the barrel and fill it up, while other merchants carefully weighed out an amount and charged by the gram). Unfortunately, stores were reluctant to return the empty firkins back to the Ljunglöf factory for recycling. The barrels were so well-built (as per Knut's high standard) that shopkeeps found infinite uses for them around the store. Even worse, some unscrupulous vendors sold the empty Ettan barrels back to other snus makers, who would fill the firkins with their own inferior product and sell it for a premium price. It is estimated that at one time, a quarter of the snus in Stockholm that was being sold as "Ettan" was actually another brand.

Ljunglöf had to search far and wide to find carpenters that could keep him steadily supplied in firkins. Unfortunately this meant that he could no longer personally inspect the quality of each barrel that he bought, and inevitably some issues cropped up. Some less-than skilled craftsmen were not sanding down and finishing the inside of their firkins, and loose sawdust was flaking off the wood and mixing in with the snus. Knut's competition took this opportunity to spread the rumor that Ettan was being mixed with sawdust in order to cut costs. This was a terrible insult to the Ljunglöfs, who had dedicated their lives to producing the best quality snus that money could buy. Indeed, even the word "Ljunglöf" was synonymous with quality- it was used as a description of premium service, much like the term "Cadillac" would come to mean that something was the best in its class.

Above: *Loading tobacco onto a rail car.*

Below: *One of Ljunglöf's barrel makers, hard at work.*

Chapter Five:
The Kingdom

SWEDEN, SWEDEN

The rumors about Ettan shook Knut to his core. They had spread beyond Sweden's borders and into Germany, where Ljunglöf had slowly been building the brand. After one Prussian retailer inquired as to whether Knut could ship his supply in a better container, Ljunglöf angrily replied that:

"...There IS no better way to export snus than the methods that I have staked my reputation on. Fresh snus was an anomaly until the advent of Ettan, and I can assure you that you will not find a fresher snus. Because, after all, fresher is better."

Until a better form of packaging was available, Knut would have to bide his time.

******

Meanwhile, throughout the rest of the nation there was something of a Swedish renaissance in motion. As a reaction to the influx of foreign trends that threatened to placate Swedish folk traditions, national romanticism in literature and the arts was at an all-time high, and quaint old peasant customs were being dusted off and revived, all in a show of Swedish pride. Taking a pinch of Ettan was as patriotic a gesture as any that had come before it.

Swedish poet and famed snuser Esias Tegner was at the forefront of the traditional Swedish movement. By protesting loudly to parliament, Tegner had saved many traditional holidays from being stricken off of the national calendar. But within a few years, the government had officially delisted over twenty such holidays amid great protest from the common folk. The people refused to conform to the new calendar. Turning to their almanacs, holiday festivals that hadn't been practiced in ages were now being celebrated by Swedes all over the country. The most popular of these celebrations was the ancient heathen holiday of Midsummer.

Left: *Knut Ljunglöf being ferried on his private boat.*

MIDSUMMER

The festivities varied in different parts of the country, but it was always a party with music and dancing. And snuff and brandy. The lyrics of "The Smaland Song" perfectly illustrate the mood of midsummer:

And the mother to her daughter, asking abruptly:
"What kind of man doesn't have snus under his lip?
Everything requires spice
the snus is like salt
And a kiss with no snus is like blood pudding with no blood!"

During the start of the festivities, the fiddler would play a jaunty tune to whip up the excitement. As the evening went on, he would begin to play slower and slower until the music took on a lazy, melancholy feel to appease the twilight, which would become longer and darker towards summer's end.

The young girls who were not yet engaged to be married picked seven kinds of flowers out of the meadow and placed them under their pillow at night. Legend had it that their future husband would be revealed to them in a dream.

But it was not just the accordion and bedsprings that got louder throughout the midsummer night. The "immoral" dances and pagan folk traditions greatly stuck in the craw of the local clergy, who would monitor the festivities until the revelers crossed whatever imaginary line that the priests had put in place. Then it was time to summon the sheriff, who would disband the party and send everyone home early. (And unlike the "hip" protestants, Catholic priests didn't pass out snus after morning service, either.)

Midsummer was also an important time of year for The Snus King. He would pack up his family and move to their summer house in Canaan. Despite its biblical name, Canaan was a raucous town where sailors could cut loose with wine, women and drink. That is, until Knut Ljunglöf showed up and demolished the local tavern/whorehouse and built his sprawling summer home on top of the rubble. He named it "White Villa."

This summer home fit in nicely with the dozens of other properties he owned around Sweden. Some were private residences, but Knut also owned several mills and game grounds that he would lease out to wealthy hunters. His most favorite hobby, however, was sailing. He took to the water every opportunity he could and loved to race his boats.

ABOVE: A MIDSUMMER PARTY AT THE LJUNGLOF ESTATE.

LEFT: TWO OF KNUT'S MANY BOATS. THE LARGER ONE WAS NAMED *TULLIA* AFTER HIS MOTHER.

The Ljunglöf saga continues next issue. Many thanks to Fredrik Olsson for additional text translation in this article.

Creepy Snuff Paraphernalia Of The Month Award

This issue's "winner":

SNUFF BOX FULL OF PUBES

Visitors to Scotland's Museum of St. Andrews University are typically unaware that the museum houses some, er, interesting artifacts not typically displayed along with the more well-known exhibits. Nay, one must have special permission to view certain objects, including the rather ordinary looking snuff box pictured here.

The tin on display was once owned by King George IV, a man known for his bawdy reputation among the ladies. He liked to keep souvenirs from his many sexual conquests, and this one happened to end up as a secret exhibit in the royal museum.

When opened, the snuff-box contains a small parchment of paper with a flowing, handwritten text. Underneath this paper is a tightly wound clump of reddish-brown human hair, approximately two inches long. The text explains that the hairs are "the Mons Veneris of a Royal Courtesan of King George IV"- that is, the pubic hair of one of King George's mistresses- lovingly clipped off and stored as a keepsake by "Dirty Georgie," as he was then called.

Apparently, snipping off your pubic hair and giving it to your lover as a gift was quite the rage in the early 18th century. A newly married couple would cut off a few hairs on their honeymoon and save them in their wedding album. Other less-romantic paramours would display the hair in their hatband as a display of their randiness or potency.

It is unclear exactly which "courtesan" donated the auburn curls in question, but it is thought that they came from Elizabeth of Coyningham, a groupie of sorts that bedded many aristocratic royals.

King George himself donated the tin as a gift to the famed pre-Victorian Edinburgh swinger's club, the Beggar's Benison, during a nostalgic 1822 visit. In years past, he spent many a night at the old club, and in his latter years he became quite sentimental over his earlier period of licentious tomcatting, remarking to a friend that if he had known that he would one day be unable to obtain an erection, he would have had even more sex in his heyday in order to make up for his later dry run.

STE

Snuffing with

Mr. Manners

YOUR GUIDE TO PROPER ETIQUETTE AND REFINED MANNERISMS WHILST PARTAKING OF SNUFF

AS DICTATED TO SETH DESJARDINS

Dear Mr. Manners,

I have heard there are a variety of fine French snuffs. Are there any you could suggest?

Remy Monteaux
Frogmore, Louisiana, USA

Dear Remy,

French snuff? FRENCH SNUFF?! My dear boy there hasn't been a single desirable thing to ever come out of France! I can only imagine if they do indeed make snuff in France (which I sincerely doubt!) it would be flavored of rotting cheese and would cause you to lament over lost love and the meaninglessness of existence.

Have you ever tried French food? Atrocious! With no ability to make edible food, how could you even propose that the French could make a satisfactory snuff?! The mere thought of those unwashed rats manufacturing snuff compels a man of virtue and stature like myself feel as if I've made eye contact with one of my servants! What a distasteful thought!

Dear Mr. Manners,

I've fancied a lady for quite some time. When I see her in social situations, I'd like to introduce myself and strike up a conversation, but I don't know what to say. Can you help me?

Richard Johnson
New Erection, Virginia, USA

Dear Richard,

Can I call you Dick? It seems like we're becoming fast friends, so I'm going to call you Dick. My my, what good friends we are becoming!

I'll get right to it then Dick, a modern lady of today desires a brutish, forceful man. It is imperative that you stare wantonly at the lady of your desire until she notices. As soon as eye contact is established, punch the man nearest to you square in the nose. Triumphant, you must then produce your snuffbox and suggestively take a manly dosage of snuff no less than one gram for each nostril. Naturally the snuff you take must be of a masculine variety such as a high dry toast. Suppress the urge to sneeze or blow your nose. The lady you desire will then clearly be smitten with your vast constitution. Make your way over to the lady and demand her company. A proper lady will acquiesce and follow your every whim. You may find she will faint from pure ecstasy after that rugged display followed by the proceeding utterance, "M'lady, I demand your company and favor! When we return to my chambers later this evening, I shall take snuff from betwixt your ample bosom!"

Dear Mr. Manners,

While enjoying a couple of brews and Bernard schmalzler with a good buddy of mine we got into a heated discussion about who had the best five year pitching performance in Major League Baseball. I said it was Pedro Martinez between the years of 1997 – 2001 and my friend said it was Sandy Kofax between 1962-1966. We agreed you'd be the final word on this debate, so which one had the better five year run?

Skip Headman
Nimrod, Minnesota, USA

Dear Skip,

I am afraid to tell you that there is so much wrong with your letter I do not know where to begin. I shall do my best to round off your sharp edges and work to make you a man of sophistication and status. It would be an injustice to you if I did not first address your choice in snuff. Schmalzler is an unrefined snuff perpetrated upon us by the Huns. A coarse and sweet mixture of what I'm assuming is sausage leavings, cabbage, molasses, dung and third rate tobacco. Good God man, if you moved in my circles and produced a snuffbox filled with schmalzler you'd be laughed out of the room, at best, if not shot on the spot. Try an SP for goodness sake!

Secondly, I am not familiar with the terms "brews" and "buddy" so I will assume that this is in reference to a strange pagan Hun ritual. I hope my response will compel you to shed the barbaric skin which you currently wear and come into the light of the modern gentleman. A dandy hat, pressed shirt, jacket and ascot will do wonders to your stature.

Finally, how dare you mention baseball! The wretched, bastard child of Cricket! All men of manners are well aware that the only genuine sports are those in which a sweater or vest is worn at all times!

Dear Mr. Manners,

Can you take snuff while driving?

Aiden Grumple
Shitlingthorpe, Yorkshire, UK

Dear Aiden,

As long as your chauffeur isn't driving erratically, I don't see why that would be a problem. For the finest and quietest ride available I suggest purchasing a 50 hp Rolls Royce, otherwise known as the *Silver Ghost*. Your snuff spoon will not be shaken asunder whilst riding in the luxurious cabin of this fine British beast! No need to worry about spilling snuff upon your jacket in this modern automobile! No sir! It bears mentioning that the chauffeur's driving bench for the Silver Ghost is on the outside of the cabin which makes for great fun during hailstorms and highwaymen robberies!

Dear Mr. Manners,

What is the sophisticated gentleman's choice for a snuffbox?

Seamus McGonigle
Muff, County Donegal, Ireland

Normally I do not make it a habit to answer queries from the Irish, but I shall make an exception. Do be so kind as to put the whiskey down long enough to absorb the breadth of my answer. There are many a fine choice in snuffbox, but any gentleman knows that your choice in this vital accessory will differentiate the everyday riff-raff from the pillars of high society.

As you may or may not be aware there are several different snuff boxes for different situations. You may notice at a social engagement that the gentleman of the house may have a fine "table box" made of a wood like mahogany with pearl or gold inlays. That is acceptable if you're only goal is to be indecipherable from the multitudes of society never-were's futilely attempting to join the truly elite. The modern man of virtue and valor knows that while a fine wooden table box is nice, the only truly elegant table box is made from a human skull adorned with jewels. Watch the envy and horror on the faces of your guest when you offer them snuff from out of a heavily jeweled human skull! If taking another man's life is not to your fancy, a viable alternative is the skull of a rare beast. You can regale your guests with a thrilling story of the hunt whilst offering them a fine snuff from the skull. There must be no more than 10 mating pairs of the animal to be an acceptable substitution for a human skull. Given these two options there is no doubt that you will astound your constituency! What better way to show that you are master of both man and beast? None, I tell you!

Outside of the home the modern gentleman needs one or more snuffboxes that are portable, durable, functional and decorative. When you access your snuffbox in public it is of utmost importance that you project an image of class and elegance. Many a man will tell you that a silver or gold snuffbox will do the trick. The more refined may even point you to a porcelain Meissen box. All three are fine choices for a modern gentleman, but there is nothing finer and more distinguished than a snuffbox fashioned from a narwhal horn. Many a fine image may be etched or painted upon a snuffbox and a narwhal horn snuffbox is no exception. Should you choose an etched box, the image must depict your superiority over all that is around you. A robust man slaying a marauding horde of heathens would do well to convey your vitality and virtue. Should you choose a painted box a softer image is in order such as said robust man romancing several women in a country garden. Any Tom, Dick or Harry can have a silver, gold or porcelain snuffbox, but they will all wilt in the aura of your narwhal horn snuffbox!

STE

Diary of a Crazy Cat Lady

By Jennifer Goldsmith

My husband rented a film the other night. (Yes, some people still do that). It was a real stinker of a suspense movie. You know the kind. There's usually a washed up character actor (Dennis Quaid) in the lead role of resident psycho. He spends the movie hamming it up and chasing after dumb teenagers. You know the kind. The ones that continuously do stupid things like poke around in the crazy man's house late at night in order to prove to everyone that he's crazy. Of course, when they try to tell the sheriff that the crazy man is killing people, the stereotypical small town sheriff does his "aw shucks, you crazy kids quit making up crazy stories 'afore I fetch your pa's to come skin yore hides" routine that date back at least to 1955's *The Blob*.

Naturally, after enough people die the crazy kids finally convince the skeptical sheriff that the crazy guy really is crazy and shenanigans ensue for about ten minutes before the film comes to its stupid, hackneyed ending that Helen Keller could have seen coming a mile away. Then we're treated to an abrupt, unnecessary epilogue where Dennis Quaid gets one more chance to overact for the camera before the credits roll.

The name of the movie is *Beneath The Darkness*, and it should be available at Red Box kiosks near you any day now. (Remember when all movies, even the really low-budget ones, had an initial theatrical release before popping up on home video? You don't? Showing my age here...) The 2011 direct-to-DVD masterpiece was filmed in Bastrop Texas, which is right outside of Austin. I know this because I had a tape- yes, an audio cassette- that my friend in Austin sent me about 15 years ago that featured a local Latino rapper bragging about how he "knew a girl in Bastrop/She can make that ass drop." (I wonder if he knew any girls from Nantucket?)

Anyway, the movie had one redeeming grace. Instead of running around smoking cigarettes through the entire film, the characters embraced the alternative tobacco culture head on. There's a scene about 39

DENNIS **QUAID**   TONY **OLLER**   AIMEE **TEEGARDEN**

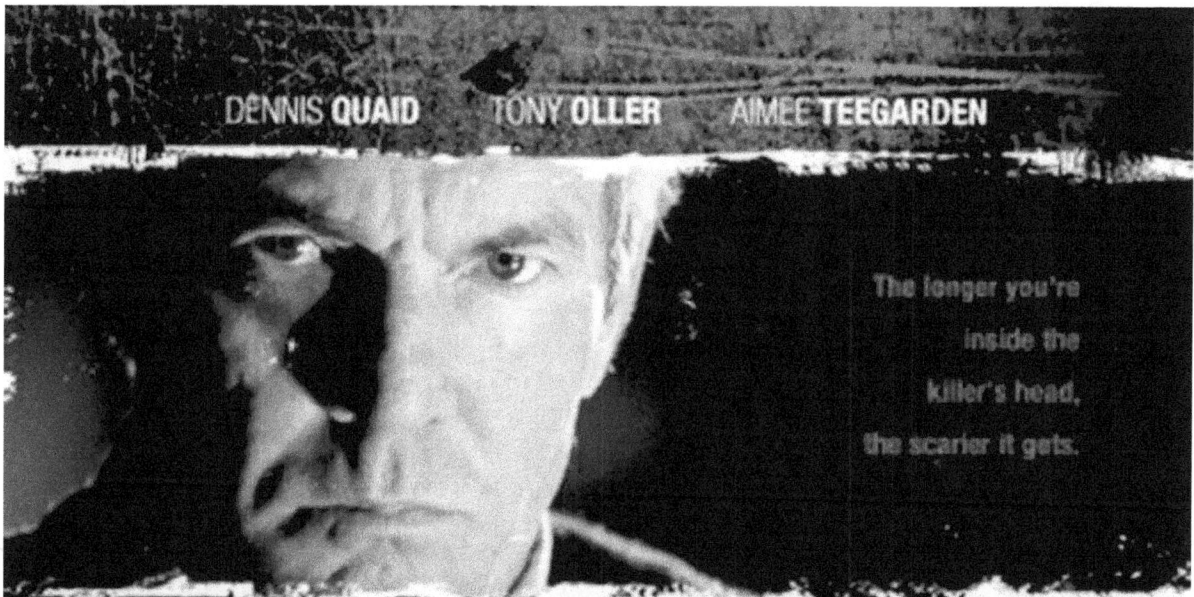

The longer you're inside the killer's head, the scarier it gets.

BENEATH the **DARKNESS**

minutes into the movie where Dennis Quaid is talking with the skeptical sheriff and he's puffing away on an E-cig. The sheriff then pulls out a can of General Onyx and lower lips the portion like a Skoal pouch. (You can even hear the distinctive "click" when he puts the lid back on the can). It came completely out of nowhere, but it rocked my socks off to see two main characters indulging in two of my habits that you never see portrayed in movies today. In fact, throughout the entire movie Dennis Quaid walks around with the E-cig in his mouth puffing away. I'm not sure which model he uses, but the indicator light flashes light blue like the Blu brand.

What's even cooler is that it's real frigging General Onyx he's using. It's not some herbal chew or loose Copenhagen tossed into the unfamiliar Onyx can. Nope, he pulls a black portion out of the can and sticks it in his mouth. No movie magic trickery there. And being that Onyx isn't even sold in America, it means that someone had to have ordered it from Sweden. Was it someone involved with the production, or was it brought to the set by the actor himself?

The guy who played the sheriff, Brett Cullen, is another one of those character actors whose name you'll never recognize but you've seen his face in a million movies. I don't know enough about his body of work or personal life to guess if he's an ex-smoker or a real snuser, but I'm going to be paying more attention whenever I come across any more

of his films. (It's funny, he looks a lot like Sean Bean to me, who is a known nasal-snuffer offscreen).

I personally think it's great to see actors embracing alternative tobacco in films. Just this week I've spotted Johnny Depp, Lindsay Lohan and Michael Beihn all smoking electronic cigarettes in movies and on TV. And let's not forget Brad Pitt's character in the recent *Inglorious Basterds* who spent the entire movie taking snuff. (I loved sitting behind the yahoos at the theater that were going "huh huh huh, he's doing blow and nobody cares! huh huh huh." These were probably the same people that thought John Travolta was rolling a joint at Jackrabbit Slim's in *Pulp Fiction*.)

On the other hand, I just watched the American remake of *The Girl With The Dragon Tattoo* and was horrified to see everyone chainsmoking through the whole film, and there was not one single solitary reference to snus even though the entire picture took place in Stockholm and Norrland. Daniel Craig even buys cigarettes at a café, which may have been possible 30 years ago, but as any real Swede could tell you, is illegal today. What's up with that? The *Millenium* films could be the ticket to introducing snus to millions of people around the world, but instead we have Daniel Craig walking into a diner and asking for a pack of Marlboro Reds by name (wonder how much Phillip Morris paid for that particular piece of product placement?) How cool would it be to see James Bond himself pull out a can of Ettan in the next movie? Come on movie industry, give Swedish Match a call next time and leave the cigarettes to pretentious hipster indie flicks.

STE

STRANGE... BUT TRUE !

TOBACCO-RELATED ODDITIES AND ANECDOTES

COMPILED BY DAVID THIGPEN

"Stop eating and start smoking" begs obesity specialist

The tiny island of Nauru is in the throes of an obesity epidemic. In fact, researches claim that it is the fattest nation in the world.

"It is interesting to note that the obesity rate started to grow in 1980, precisely the time when our government persuaded the majority of people to stop smoking," claims Balthar Quinon, national health specialist. "But far from becoming a healthier populace, we have instead become obese and deadly."

When asked if he thought that the nation would be better off as smokers, Quinon didn't mince words. "Of course! Being overweight is much more dangerous than smoking. If we were to all stop eating the western diet and take back up cigarettes, then our weight would decrease and our instances of heart disease would also reduce." As for the threat of lung cancer, don't fret: "The lung cancer rate in smokers is less than 10 percent. The heart attack rate for the morbidly obese is over 90 percent."

A BRAIN FULL OF SCORPIONS

The basil herb was once one of the more common ingredients in snuff, although its use in modern snuff making is limited to mostly Indian brands. Its loss in popularity may be attributed to an old wive's tale that began circulating in the late 17th century.

According to legend, an Italian peasant snuffed basil-laced tobacco continuously until one day, he became stark-raving mad. He collapsed and died, and a post-mortem removal of his skull revealed a nest of scorpions living in his brain, apparently having been born of the snuff.

Similar tales about scorpions and basil date back to the time of Christ. The Greeks believed it to be an aphrodisiac, and while planting it, would rant and curse loudly. This was thought to increase the plant's potency.

Edgar Cayce's SNUFF Tin Prophecies

Certainly one of the most unique individuals to have ever been part of our little community of snuff takers had to have been Edgar Cayce.

Born in 1877, the mild mannered southerner would fall into a deep trance-like state and give psychic readings that ranged from the mundane to the extraordinary. Most of his predictions were, like those of Nostradamus, vague enough to be interpreted a number of different ways, although he occasionally displayed moments of seemingly-genuine clairvoyance.

"The Sleeping Prophet," as he was called, lived in constant conflict with his trance predictions. A devout Christian who regularly taught Sunday school, Cayce was dismayed when his readings began taking an Eastern tinge by including references to past lives and reincarnation. Cayce himself wondered if he may have been possessed by demons. Nevertheless, Cayce continued to give readings free of charge up until his death in 1945.

A few years ago, a guy popped up claiming to have unearthed a slew of prophecies written by Cayce before his death and hidden inside one of his empty snuff tins. This discovery was even more miraculous in that it was allegedly found inside the rubble of the World Trade Center. (How the tin arrived at the WTC or how it survived the wreckage of the 9/11 attacks has yet to be explained.)

The time frame of the predictions begins with the September 11th, 2001 terrorist attacks in New York and finishes off in 2013, earth's "final year." A brief sampling of some of the prophecies:

- Dolphins are secretly communicating with extraterrestrials in a plan to destroy mankind.

- Evil robots will take over Japan.

- People will discover an ancient chant that allows them to remain young forever- that is, until Christian scientists realize that the chant is satanic and dooms anyone who has uttered it to an eternity in hell.

- The Chinese will prove that America has never been to the moon when they land there and discover no evidence of mankind having ever touched down.

- In 2010, the earth's axis will shift making the North Pole south and the South Pole north. Reverse polarity ensues.

- Venus will vanish forever.

- Demonic sightings are rampant, and millions of Christians kill themselves to avoid living in a world controlled by Satan.

- A race of genetically modified super-savages are being created in South America with telepathic abilities that will render homo sapiens obsolete.

- America elects a communist president in 2009. He is then accidentally killed by his grandson, who was playing with a loaded gun.

- "Evil foreigners from middle lands" kill millions of Americans in Chicago, New York and Hamlet, NC. But a bunch of angels come from the sky and bring everyone back to life.

- Christ returns to earth to battle Adolf Hitler, who is now working for the antichrist.

- After the axis shift, America and Europe will be continentally side-by-side and Florida and California fall into the ocean.

- **Remember, all of these things are supposed to happen by next year, so be prepared.**

URBAN LEGEND DEPARTMENT

Nicolaxx Anal Suppositories: The Legend That Just Won't Die

What started out as a viral spoof on the IamLost website over ten years ago is still running strong. At first glance, the ad looks legit until you read the copy:

Nicolaxx is quite easy to administer and quitting smoking has never been this easy! Remove the wrapper and moisten the Nicolaxx Suppository with cool water. If the suppository is too soft to use, we recommend putting it in the refrigerator for about 15 minutes. After you are ready, Lie down on your side and use your fingers to push the pointed end of the Nicolaxx Suppository well up into the rectum.

Nicolaxx
Nicotine Anal Suppositories

And the kicker:

The reuse of a Nicotine Anal Suppositories after a bowel movement is not recommended. We recommend using a new Nicolaxx suppository after your bathroom visit is completed.

We get at least one email per week along the lines of "OMG- You should put that Nicolaxx crap in the SBT section!" (*sigh*) or "Have you seen this yet?" (*yes, about 40,000 times*).

Like all good urban legends, this one has a ring of truth to it. Tobacco suppositories were used by the Indians to bring on spiritual hallucinations and during the 17th century, Europeans thought that a tobacco enema was great for clearing out the pipes. And lets not forget that guy in Sweden that recently stuck three cans of snus in his rectum.

This story, however, is [insert fecal waste matter joke here].

Niggas Either Winnin', Pimpin' or Runnin' Thangs: The Mythology of Newport

Next to Marlboro and Camel, no other cigarette brand has spawned as many urban legends and conspiracy theories as Newport. Let's look at just a few of the many crazy rumors attached to 'Ports.

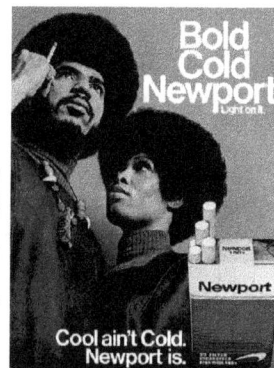

- Newports are owned by the KKK and are being marketed and sold to minorities for the sole purpose of eradicating them.
- Newports have been bought by Jay-Z (or another rap mogul) and officially stand for "Niggaz Either Winning, Pimpin' or Running Thangz."
- Newports contain fiberglass.
- Newports contain Yellow #5, the same insidious ingredient found in Mountain Dew that is supposed to make black men sterile.
- There's a secret Newport giveaway going on. If you tear open the bottom of your pack and see the letters "WN" followed by a number, it means you've "won" that many free packs (or cartons).
- NEWPORT is an acronym for a pornographic slogan.
- Barack Obama smokes Newports (*he smokes Marlboro*).
- Malcolm X smoked Newports (*he smoked Lucky Strikes*).
- Colin Powell smoked Newports (*nope, Marlboro Lights*).
- When you fold the top of a Newport box backwards, you'll find a secret hole that you can rest your cigarette in. This is so that you can keep your cigarette burning while you smoke weed (or crack) and it will mask the smell of the burning drugs.
- Newports were originally launched as a non-menthol brand marketed to upscale, white 50's America. (*This one is actually true. The menthol version came later and Lorillard didn't begin marketing the brand to blacks until the 1970s.*)
- The KKK owns Newport, and the brand name indicates their desire to turn America into one giant new slave port.
- Newports contain a secret ingredient used to hook black smokers on menthol.
- Newports contain much more menthol than other brands. This is to ensure that it causes a black smoker's lungs to bleed profusely.
- Newports contain a secret ingredient created by jealous whites that will shrink the size of a black man's penis.
- The filter on a Newport will cause toxic shock syndrome in black smokers, causing their lips to swell to cartoonish proportions.

SHIRLEY, THE CHAIN-SMOKING ORANGUTAN

Malaysia, keeper of the world's cruelest zoos, is home to Shirley the Orangutan, an ape that draws visitors from all over Asia. When she's not busy chewing on aluminum cans or other waste items that spectators toss into her cage, she's busy smoking up to three packs worth of cigarettes a day.

It's not quite clear when Shirley began smoking, but she's obviously long enough in the habit to toss out brands that she doesn't like. (Her favorites are Marlboro and Stuyvesant.) She can work a lighter and matches, but she prefers to light up with the smoldering butt of a soon-to-expire cigarette she has just finished; the classic trait of a chain smoker.

Her visitors repeatedly ignore the signs on her cage forbidding them to give her cigarettes, and often toss full packs into her cage, which she effortlessly opens and puffs away. Zookeepers daily confiscate any lighters or matches they find in her cage, but noted that "she hides them so well, they're hard to ban completely."

FROM THE ARCHIVES: 1934

BABY SMOKES CORNCOB USED BY GRANDFATHER

PITTSBURGH -- Two-and-a-half-year-old Mickey Baehr's favorite pastime is smoking his grandfather's corncob pipe —which is plenty strong.

The pipe prodigy, whose parents live on Pittsburgh's north side, comes from a long line of smokers.

On the feminine side, his great-grandmoaher aged 103 still smokes regularly.

The child's father, W. J. Baehr, said Mickey learned to smoke by soothing his gums on the corncob while the grandfather nodded in his chair. He had formed the habit before he was found out.

"If you want to see him raise a rumpus," said the father, "just try to take the pipe away from him."

Electronic Cigarette Explodes in Man's Face

Florida native Tom Holloway received an unpleasant surprise this Valentine's Day when his e-cig's battery exploded in his mouth, knocking out all of his teeth and melting off part of his tongue.

The 64 year old father of three stopped smoking two years ago due to problems with his lungs, and turned to e-cigs, a much safer alternative to traditional tobacco cigarettes.

His wife reported hearing a loud bang, like a firecracker, coming from his study. She rushed in to find the room on fire and her husband lying on the floor, blood streaming out of his mouth.

Although it was impossible to determine the brand of e-cig Holloway was using, investigators blamed the faulty lithium battery for overheating and then exploding.

Though this is the first reported case of a non-modified electronic cigarette blowing up, thousands of similar explosions occur every year from cell phones equipped with the same type of lithium ion battery. At least 200 deaths have been attributed worldwide to rechargeable cellular phone battery explosions.

Holloway is reportedly in stable condition, though his family says that he will need extensive dental work and plastic surgery before he will be able to return home.

Oral Sex: More Dangerous Than Oral Tobacco

According to a worldwide coalition of physicians, scientists, researchers and epidemiologists, tobacco is no longer the leading cause of oral cancer in adults under 50. The new danger? Human Papilloma Virus- more commonly known as HPV.

The virus is mainly spread through oral sex and has long been known to be a risk factor for cervical cancer among women; almost 70% of all intrauterine cancers are caused by HPV.

For decades, about 90% of all reported cases of throat and mouth cancer could directly be attributed to smoking and alcohol use. But in the last twenty years, researchers say that oral cancers began to rise dramatically among people aged 20 or younger- most of whom had never used alcohol or tobacco before.

In England, cases of throat cancer have risen sharply. In the US, the incidence of oral cancers linked to HPV have doubled in the last 20 years. In Sweden forty years ago, around a quarter of tonsil cancers were linked to HPV, but that figure today has risen to 90%.

Someone infected with HPV 16 - the strain linked to oral cancer- has a 14 fold increase in risk for getting oropharynx cancer, according to Professor Maura Gillison of the University of Ohio (Columbus). "What is most strongly linked to oral HPV infection is the number of sexual partners someone has had in their lifetimes, in particular the number of individuals on whom they have performed oral sex. The higher the number of partners that you've had, the greater the odds that you'd have an oral infection."

Last year a study at Johns Hopkins University found that HPV posed a greater risk in contracting cancer than smoking or alcohol. The study showed that those with more than six sex partners were almost nine times at greater risk of contracting the disease.

Most HPV infections have no symptoms and people often do not need treatment. In America, an estimated 85% of the 20 million people living with HPV have no idea that they've contracted the disease.

Editor's note: *We can't wait to see the type of warning labels that the FDA is going to require young adults to tattoo on their genitals.* **"This Penis Can Cause Gum Disease and Tooth Loss"** *has a particularly nice ring to it, as does* **"This Vagina Is Not A Safe Alternative To Cigarettes."** STE

What Would Jesus Do?

COMMENTARY BY BILL JOHNSON

Ye publisher tells me I get a lot of mail wanting to know about my personal beliefs and whatnot. I'm fine sharing a few details here and there, but I'm careful to divulge certain tidbits because I don't want to come across as an a-hole like Andy Rooney or a pompous windbag (take your pick from any of the morbidly obese political commentators in the media today) and really, who cares about what some retired nut like me has to say about the price of tea in China?

Religion, like sex and politics, remains one of those "taboo" topics that people don't discuss in polite company. I talk with my friends when we go fishing or hunting about certain things that I don't address in public, and it's these things that the fellows behind this magazine want me to discuss in my columns. "Don't worry if you offend anyone. Hell, *try* to offend everyone!" they tell me. Junior Walter Winchells, they are.

So this column is sort of about religion, and it will probably make a few people mad. So as a forewarning, if you're easily offended by Christianity in general or theological dissection of the historical Jesus, you might want to skip this one.

OK, one more thing before I get into the nuts and bolts of this discourse. Yes, I am a Christian. I go to church on most Sundays. I'm a protestant, though I don't belong to any particular branch. (My current church is Presbyterian, but it could just as easily be Methodist or Baptist. It happens to be the closest one to my house.) I do believe the bible is sometimes meant to be taken literally and sometimes figuratively, and the problem with most religions is when one guy stands up and goes "*God* was trying to say such and such in this verse" instead of saying "I *think* God was trying to say this, but the ambiguity of the wording probably means it should be interpreted by the reader and not some dandy in the pulpit."

So I guess you can say I'm skeptical of all aspects of Christianity aside from Christ himself. This puts me at odds with a lot of the preachers I've known throughout my life. There's been some real turds that have taken up the cloth in my experience.

One of these fellows was a guy I'll call "The Country Club Preacher." This jerk was a red-faced, retired army sergeant or something that realized he could save a bunch of money on his taxes by switching to Jesus. He would do his two hours on Sunday and the rest of the week he'd be at the country club playing golf. Church rotary meetings usually centered around him trying to shake the church down for more money to send his kids to college or finance his Jaguar. And it was all because "Gawwwd told me to come before you today and make my needs known." Unfortunately, Gawwwd didn't warn him that the church was going to vote him out after about two months and hire a lower-maintenance preacher instead.

But before Mr. Country Club got kicked off the island, he delivered a sermon about Christ's miracle in Cana, the wedding he was at where he turned the water into wine. It was going pretty good until he got to the part where he said "and unlike the Catholics, we know the type of wine they're talking about in the bible was non-alcoholic." Well, I'm not Catholic but this was sure news to me. I looked around at the people sitting in the pews and it looked like it was news to them as well. Mr. Country Club sensed everyone's puzzlement and so he went on to describe that the wine of the bible was unfermented, therefore it was non-alcoholic grape juice.

Well, I had never heard this before, so I went to the library downtown and got a couple of books about the bible and the history of wine, and I realized that the preacher was full of it. I even called my second cousin, a Southern Baptist Free Will preacher, and asked him about it. His opinion was unequivocal: "That guy's full of hockey." (Preachers down south are known to talk nasty when it comes to certain subjects-misconstruction of the Scriptures being the main one).

According to one of my books, it seems that this misconception started during the Temperance movement way back in the 1800s. These know-it-alls that were trying

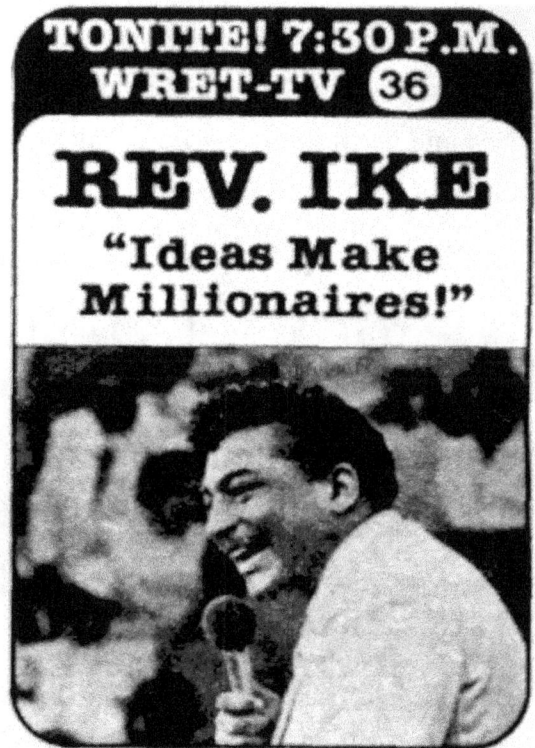

Clearly, the world needs less Billy Grahams and more Reverend Ikes.

to convince everyone to stop drinking in the name of the Lord had one problem- if Jesus drank wine, how is alcohol a sin? Their solution was to turn that wine into grape juice- a miracle to rival even Christ's feat.

But there's a couple of problems with that. If all the wine in the bible were actually grape juice, how would you explain the groom's father praising Jesus for his impeccable taste in spirits: "And he said to him, 'Every man at the beginning sets out the good wine, and when the guests are well drunk, then the inferior. You have kept the good wine until now!'" (John 2, Verses 1-10). How would the guests get "well drunk" off non-alcoholic grape juice?

Jesus taught that wine with your meal or at a festivity was beneficial, but warned not to become a drunkard. These same old teachings were continued by the Apostle Paul, who told Timothy to drink a little bit of wine for his health, but later warns the Corinthians not to drink *too* much wine at Passover, drunkenness being a sin. The bible never tells anyone to completely abstain from alcohol unless they have a problem with it. Or, if their moderate consumption would potentially cause their brothers to sin, it is best to not consume alcohol in the presence of that person.

Most of this is common sense. A little wine is healthy, which is why Christ and his followers drank it (as did pretty much everyone else in the Old and New Testaments). Drinking too much will lead you to sin (drunkenness, licentious behavior, etc). Drinking too often is gluttony, and a sign of alcoholism (definitely not a behavior tolerated by God). And even though you have no problem drinking a glass or two at dinner, you certainly wouldn't pop open a brewski in the presence of your drunk uncle Charlie, who just got his 90 day AA token for the thirtieth time.

"I've got the nickel if thou hast the dime," Paul wrote to Timothy. "Let's get together and buy a little wine."

Keeping Fit -:-

By E. ELLIOTT RAWLINS, M. D.

Jazz--a Drug

Morphine, cocaine and opium are powerful drugs which can be used for relief of pain. They are used only in this legitimate way by the guidance of a physician, for a definite purpose only. In any other way they are useless and harmful, and their sale and use are specifically determined by law. This is not so with jazz. The form of music called jazz is just as intoxicating as morphine or cocaine; it is just as harmful, and yet its use is not determined by law.

In my opinion, the bible teaches that consumables such as food and alcohol are neutral, and through our free will we either use them beneficially or abuse them self-destructively. A McDonald's hamburger is no more sinful than a red apple, but if you eat forty Big Macs a day you're going to wind up in a world of hurt. Hey, you'll die from drinking too much water or breathing too much air, and I don't see anyone rushing to ban those.

So I try to apply this philosophy to all of our human creature comforts. When I was growing up, morphine addiction was fairly common. The generation before me had been to World War One and had in turn got blown up, shot and gassed to hell and back by the Germans. The unimaginably excruciating pain that they must have gone through was greatly aided by battlefield injections of morphine. A century before, these same fellows would have been scrambling for a loaded musket so they could blow their brains out rather than endure another minute of the horrendous pain they felt.

But when they got back home, they continued to shoot up even though their wounds had long since healed. These weren't skid row junkies digging between their toes to find an untapped vein; these were farmers and blacksmiths who worked every day to feed their families and at the end of the day "took a sleeve" and slept peacefully throughout the night. Today, we would call these men "hopeless addicts" and throw them in jail for sixty years, but in my day they taught Sunday school and lead productive lives without ever falling into the decrepit pit of deadly behavior that we associate with intravenous drug use.

And what of those other two social drug

MAGEE, MARSHALL & Co., Ld.,
BOLTON.

HEALTH GIVING
COCA WINE

FOR FATIGUE OF MIND AND BODY.
GUARANTEED ABSOLUTELY PURE.

THIS Wine is most beneficial in cases where the stomach is weak, being absolutely free from Tannin. M., M. & Co. have given special attention to the production of a Coca Wine of highest quality, which will justify the recommendation of any medical man. M., M. & Co.'s Coca Wine is the most powerful nerve tonic of the day. It increases the appetite, promotes digestion, and produces sound and refreshing sleep, without the distressing feelings so often experienced after taking Opiates, Hydrate of Chloral, Bromides, &c. Coca Wine is invaluable as a strengthening medicine. It relieves nervous debility, quenches thirst, and strengthens the mental and physical powers.

One Wine-glassful Coca Wine represents one dram of Erythroxylon Coca Leaves.

DOSE AS A TONIC.---One Wine-glassful before or with each meal.
Children Half or Quarter of a Wine-glassful.

MAGEE, MARSHALL & Co Ltd, Bolton & Wigan.

perennials, marijuana and cocaine? Hell, when I was a kid reefer grew wild in the country and all along the railroad tracks. Hobos would smoke it in lieu of liquor and nobody thought anything of it. Cocaine was something less common, but we all knew what it was. Back then it was a drug associated mainly with black people, but again nobody thought much of it. I read now about the anti-drug reforms that were going on in the northern cities and the terrors of the "cocaine epidemic" and "marijuana madness" that gripped the country and I have to chuckle. None of that happened down south. The "drug crazed negroes" of Chicago should have come to North Carolina. They wouldn't have been hassled down here!

In fact, the two most "scandalous" drugs I remember when I was a kid were moonshine and ether. Moonshine was taboo because the people making it were usually the trashiest hillbilly rednecks this side of *Deliverance* and wouldn't hesitate to blow your head off if you looked at them funny. If you showed up at a party with a jug of moonshine, it meant you were a "bad dude" who had some unsavory friends, and chances are nobody messed with you.

Ether, on the other hand, was controversial just because it was what old ladies got high off of. There was an old widow women down the road from us named Mrs. Johnson (no relation) who would talk to herself and chase imaginary squirrels with her broomstick off the front porch. As kids, we would all gather round when the grocery boy would drop off her weekly commodities, because we all knew that within an hour she was going to start rag huffing that ether and putting on a show for the whole county to see.

So I guess my point is that I grew up in an era where drugs were common place and didn't become a "problem" until the bigwigs started running around banning everything that brought people comfort. And I see this same thing going on now with tobacco. But my argument to that is that if Jesus and his people drank wine, why can't we have tobacco? The knee-jerk reaction is that "tobacco is deadly," but as we all know this is pretty inaccurate a statement. In fact, I maintain that if tobacco were commonplace among the Jews 2,000 years ago, Jesus would have been using it along with his wine.

Before you think I'm speaking blasphemy or just off my rocker, consider my history. I've tried alcohol exactly once in my life and it just wasn't for me. But I believe that I get the same benefits from those who drink the occasional beer or four without the after effects of a hangover or a lifetime of 12 stepping. Just as alcohol has the power to heal, sooth, meditate, tranquilize and "spice up" an otherwise mundane activity, so to does tobacco.

Our Amerindian ancestors began smoking tobacco roughly at the same time that Noah was getting drunk off the very first wine batch (if you believe what the Old Testament says). Like Noah, or whomever fermented that first gallon of grape juice, the first person to stick a piece of tobacco in his mouth and chew on it probably ignored the bitter taste and focused more on the buzz he was getting. And after thousands of years of experimentation, humans had discovered different methods of making alcohol just as the early Americans had devised a myriad of ways to grow and consume tobacco.

Let's look at the varieties of alcohol that were known in Christ's time, and were presumably available for consumption in his neck of the woods. That section of the middle east was smack in the middle of the imperial trade route that brought customs and goods from all over the world into the neighborhoods and towns that Christ grew up in. This would have meant that he would have had an ample selection of beverages to choose from. In addition to the common wine, there was beer, mead, and cider. "Sweet wines," made from wild fruits and berries, were low in alcohol and comparable to today's wine coolers. The Romans had also apparently developed distilled liquor by then, but its extent of use is unknown.

Each culture had attached their own prejudices and affinities to the different classes of alcohol. Wine, as they say, was all things to all men. From the lowliest shepherd to the most noble of royalty, wine was the universal beverage of the time and saw no real class distinction.

Sweet wines, on the other hand, were usually associated more with the peasant class. It was much easier to go and pick a bunch of wild berries than it was to tend to a personal vinyard, so these drinks were quite common among the less-wealthy. In the upper strata of society, sweet wine was usually given to children or pregnant women.

"One day," *Chief Lefthand said before passing the pipe,* "greedy white man will manufacture his own tobacco. But then he will be ruled by other greedy white men, and they will raise price of tobacco so high that he come crawling back to reservation in search of big bargain." *The other scouts nodded in understanding.* "Then we scalp him. Or take all his money in casino. Whichever more painful."

Cider was not very common, and cost a pretty good bit of money compared to the other types. It had a reputation as an "artisans" drink, and was usually reserved for very special occasions.

Beer was the lowest common denominator in the food chain. Back then, it was associated with drunkenness and vagrancy. While one drank wine for religious ceremonies, one drank beer to get tore up. Mead was held in a slightly higher regard, but was much less common than beer. Liquor, if it was even known to the Nazarenes, would have certainly belonged to this same class.

Jesus's admiration for wine was pretty telling of the type of message he tried to convey. By abstaining from beer and mead it was like he was saying "stay away from hard drinks". Conversely, by not drinking the cheaper, low alcohol sweet wine, he seemed to be saying that a moderately high alcohol content was important for therapeutic reasons.

The status of wine as both a drink of men and a drink of kings fits in nicely with Jesus's dual nature, having referred to himself alternately as the Son of Man and the Son of God. Christ, our King of Kings, lowered himself to servant status by humbling himself on the cross. If he were trying to emphasize his magnificence at the Cana wedding, he would have turned the water into cider. Instead, in a show of modesty, he created wine instead.

So how would Jesus have preferred his tobacco, based on his choice in alcohol? This is basically the same argument that I heard some folks talking about at a restaurant a few years back. They wondered what type of vehicle Jesus would drive. "A minivan, so he could fit all the apostles inside," said one woman. "A hybrid," said another, "because he loved the earth." Another fellow said a motorcycle, since after all, "Jesus was a rebel." (I personally think he would have driven an old Buick, but that's just because I like old Buicks).

Now let's say that Jesus had all the tobacco we have at our disposal now: dry or moist snuff, cigarettes, cigars and pipe tobacco. (I'm going to ignore chewing tobacco and stuff like dissolvables and orbs. Swedish snus/snuff should be included along with moist snuff for sake of this argument).

First off, since cigarettes are clearly addictive to most people and cause the most amount of damage to the body, I seriously doubt Christ would have had a Camel hanging out of his mouth while he conferred with Pontius Pilate. No, cigarettes are the beer and whiskey of the tobacco realm. Cheap and dirty, designed to give you a buzz and send you on your way. Oh sure, you can buy some premium cigarettes and rolling tobacco, but like honey mead it's only marginally better than the regular stuff. Jesus would not have been a cigarette smoker.

Well, what about cigars? And I'm not talking the two for a nickel strawberry stinkers they keep next to the cash register at the gas station. I'm talking about the real, hand rolled stogies that help you smell a rich man walking from a mile away. Cigars are now, and have really always been, a costume prop for the wealthy. If you wanted to impress a gold digger, you would stick a hundred dollar Havana in your mouth and puff away like a moron. And again, if Jesus would have wanted to display this type of image, he would have been drinking cider instead of wine.

This leaves us with pipe tobacco and snuff. Now, as much as I love all the various types of wet snuff out there and all the new (to me) brands of Swedish snus that they send me, I have to admit that the main reason most of us probably use this stuff is because we're chasing a nicotine buzz. I wouldn't recommend that anyone stick a piece of snus or chewing snuff in his mouth unless he's prepared to repeat that procedure another 6 billion times over the course of his lifetime. Even though the effect on your body will be pretty minimal, I just don't see Jesus advocating something that so many people find addictive.

So between dry nasal snuff and pipe smoking, who would win? Like wine, snuffing and piping have a long, traditional history behind them. They've both been used widely by both the wealthy and the common. They're both out of favor now compared to cigarettes and cigars, just as beer and liquor both gradually supplanted wine in popularity.

Snuff and pipe smoking contain healthy amounts of nicotine, but not an egregious amount like cigarettes or a negligible amount like a cigar. Table wine (like Jesus drank) wasn't high proof like beer, neither was it a child's drink like sweet wine.

Wine is considered healthy by most doctors and they recommend a glass or two at dinner for a variety of reasons. Until a few years ago, doctors recommended smoking a pipe for the very same reason. Just as you're probably not going to get liver disease from drinking a glass a day, you're probably not going to get mouth or throat cancer from smoking a pipebowl a day. The key word here again is "moderation."

Unfortunately in this day and age, snuffing isn't anywhere near as widely practiced as pipe smoking, and so it's a custom that's is pretty alien to most of society. On the other hand, most any old fart like me can light up a pipe and unless you were raised communist, you'll be blessed with the pleasant memories of your grandpa or father smoking their pipes and the sweet smell that went along with it.

But pop open a tin of snuff and take a healthy whiff and they'll think you're one of those "drug crazed negroes" from Chicago that's come to blow cocaine all over them. That's not usually the case with pipe tobacco, unless you live in New York where just *thinking* about nicotine will get you the death penalty.

And so for this reason, I have to give the prize to the pipe. But if we were going by the standards of a couple of hundred years ago when snuffing was commonplace and indoor pipe smoking was considered rude, then I 'd

have definitely gone with snuff.

Of course, this whole argument is kind of moot anyway, since Jesus never smoked a pipe that we know of and speculating about it is just a waste of time. But when you're my age, you think of some crazy things when you're all alone, sitting on the couch wishing your cat would wake up so you'd have somebody to talk to. Have you noticed how terrible daytime television is? I have 400 channels and the best I can come up with is reruns of 50 year old *Combat!* episodes. Kind of makes me wish I had some morphine.

sᴛᴇ

Bill Johnson once unsuccessfully sued Ol' Dirty Bastard for stealing his nickname.

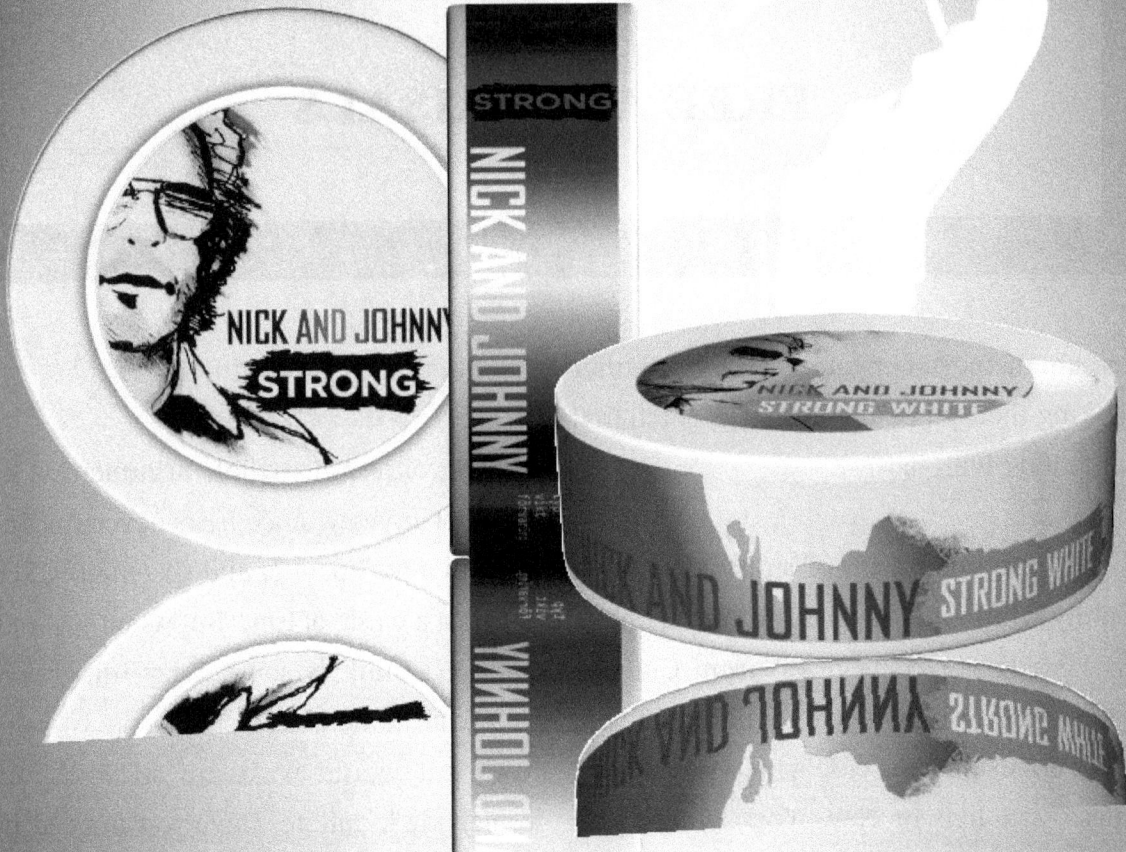

www.snuscentral.com   f www.facebook.com/snuscentral

SNUS GALLERY

(Left:) Tobacco-rette
Snus, a Zimbabwe br
(www.nandb.co.zw/t
corette. html)

(Below:) Lindgrens S
"Make Your Own" Ki
(www.lindgrenssnus

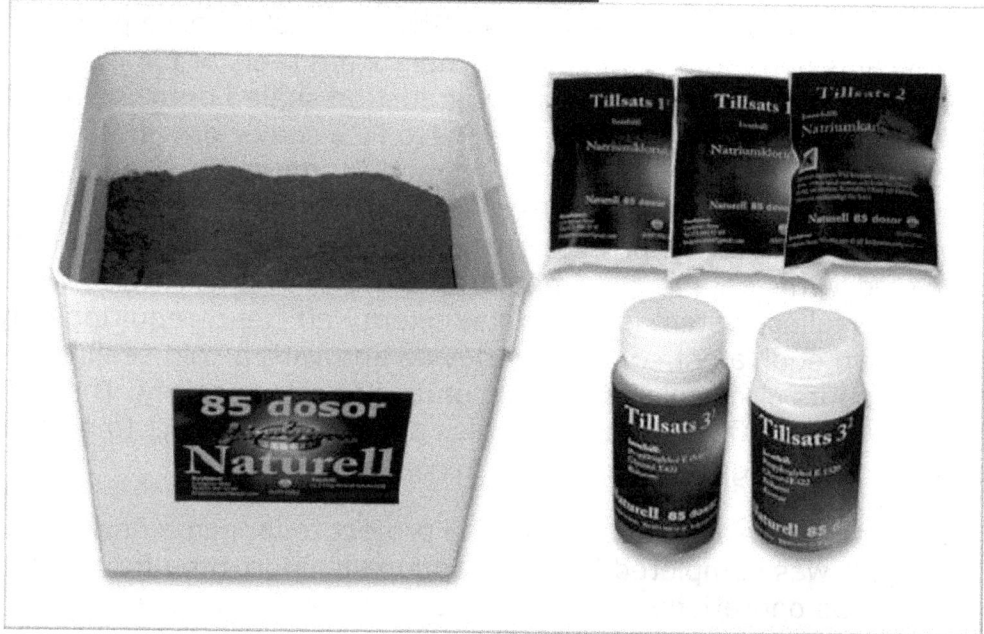

Random Stuff We Found Online

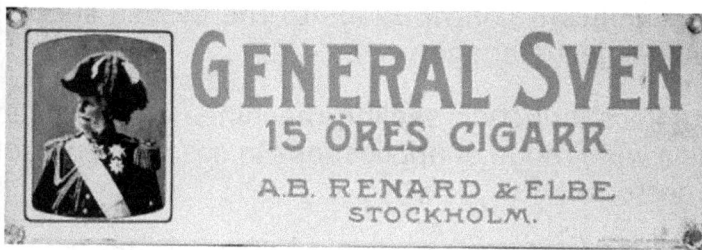

GENERAL SVEN
15 ÖRES CIGARR
A.B. RENARD & ELBE
STOCKHOLM.

(Left:) Renard & Elbe Snus
Manufacturer, Stockholm-
Tin Sign- Ca. 1856

*Non-credited photos courtesy
of The Swedish Tobacco
Museum (www. Tobaks
ochtandsticksmuseum. se/en)

Relco Press Release:
Lucky Strike Snus Foil System
December 21st, 2005

www.relco.co.uk/press_release/
LuckyStrike.htm

Custom built foiling system for Lucky Strike 'Snus' tobacco pouches

Relco, the UK based designer and manufacturer of induction and RF sealing machinery have produced a custom built foiling system especially for British American Tobacco's new line of Lucky Strike 'Snus' tobacco pouches. The cutting of the seal is done to a print register mark from reels of foil in order to provide a label effect seal before being directly induction sealed onto the tin-plate can. The quality of the result achieved by the Relco FCS sealer provides a hermetic seal to preserve freshness which has an attractive appearance and is also easy for customers to remove. Working from reel-fed material stock is considerably more economical than using pre-cut magazine fed seals and avoids the problems associated with feeding thin membranes from a stack. Relco's unique capless induction sealing system is also highly energy efficient, requiring only 20% of the power of an equivalent conduction device and with a cold sealing head, provides added benefits of cleanliness and increased operator safety. The in-house design and development facilities at Relco also allowed the project to be completed from concept to working machine in just 12 weeks.

"The machine was ordered as part of a project to launch a new product category. The project was completed in an exceptionally short time frame, and the sealing machine was operational within two days of arriving at the factory. RELCO were very committed to the project and provided invaluable advice and assistance not only on the sealing machine, but also on packaging design and materials selection, both of which have made significant contributions to the overall success of this project." A.N.Robinson BAT Project Manager.

The Relco FCS range of capless induction sealing machines can be used on any container material and has a wide range of applications in cosmetic, personal care, food and pharmaceutical sectors.

Lucky Strike is a trademark of British American Tobacco (Brands) Inc.

FRISKENS Stjernsnus är bäst.

FABRIKS MÄRKE · FRISK · 1901

AKTIEBOLAGET
ERIC MELLGREN & SON
SNUS & TOBAK

SNUSFABRIKEN STOCKHOLM

KING

PORTION

(Above:) Friskens Star Snus, Mellgren & Son Snus tin signs (ca. 1860)

(Left:) King Snus, 2005 proposed can design (patriksundbergdesign.com/Snus.htm)

(Below:) Pick Brand Snus, Ca. 1890

BRAND
SNUS

PICK BRAND

Snus, Taxes and the Moral Traveler

commentary by
Anthony Haddad

I have a few rules for travel destinations that drive my wife nuts. But I think it speaks to my deeply held moral convictions as well as her moral relativism.

For example, I won't visit a country that doesn't have strip clubs. I don't visit these clubs often, but any country that gets in the way of such a straightforward and honest business deal is horrible. Some women need money, and some men need boobs rubbed on their faces.

Similarly, I am deeply suspicious of any country that doesn't have a homegrown porn industry. All it takes is a cheap camera and a little cash. If no one can get that together or someone is stopping them, I call shenanigans.

Countries without a local tradition of liquor, beer or wine production are out, too. And if drinking is illegal, forget about it -- that's not a holiday, it's a prison term.

Similarly, if you can't bring snus, it's out. I don't care if I have to pay to bring it in. I ain't moving there, so I'm not worried about tax rates and local sales laws -- even though sales bans are patently horseshit.

But if you are moving somewhere, it matters a lot. I've crunched the numbers for the U.S. and the best states for liquor and snus are Arizona, Kansas, Kentucky, Maryland, Missouri, South Carolina, Tennessee, West Virginia, Wyoming, and Washington, D.C. All these states have liquor and snus tax rates that are less than half the national average of $6.35 per gallon for liquor and $0.90 per 24 grams for snus.

Liquor taxes range from nothing in Wyoming and New Hampshire to $26.45 a gallon in Washington state -- more than 4 times the national average. Snus taxes range from nothing in Pennsylvania to $2.30 a tin in Wisconsin -- more than 2.5 times the national average. Of course, these tax rates probably aren't enough to make it worth packing up and moving across the country. But it's something you should keep in mind when you do move.

For example, I'd never move to Washington or Oregon. It's rainy, so I'd likely drink more, and my booze would end up costing me an extra $1,000 a year. Similarly, I'm interested in getting out of Texas. It's hot, the snus tax here probably costs me $500 a year, and all the strippers have beer bellies and sideburns. STE

When Anthony Haddad isn't stuffing dollar bills into various orifices, he blogs snus over at DrSnus.com. His new book, Drink Thin, *is available on Amazon (and probably a few other places too- we don't really feel like checking.)*

Alcohol and Tobacco Tax Rates By State*

State	Liquor Tax, by gallon	Smokeless tobacco tax, per 24 grams	State	Liquor Tax, by gallon	Smokeless tobacco tax, per 24 grams
Alabama,AL	*$18.78*	**$0.01**	*Nebraska,NE*	$ 3.75	**$0.37**
Alaska,AK	*$12.80*	*$1.73*	Nevada,NV	$ 3.60	$0.69
Arizona,AZ	**$ 3.00**	**$0.20**	*New Ham.,NH*	**$ 0.00**	*$1.10*
Arkansas,AR	**$ 2.58**	*$1.56*	New Jersey,NJ	$ 5.50	$0.64
California,CA	$ 3.30	$0.76	*New Mex,NM*	$ 6.06	$0.58
Colorado,CO	**$ 2.28**	*$0.92*	*New York,NY*	*$ 6.44*	*$2.00*
Connecti.,CT	$ 4.50	$0.85	*North Ca.,NC*	*$13.39*	**$0.29**
Delaware,DE	$ 5.46	$0.46	North Dak,ND	**$ 2.50**	$0.51
Florida,FL	*$ 6.50*	*$1.96*	*Ohio,OH*	*$ 9.04*	**$0.39**
Georgia,GA	$ 3.79	**$0.23**	*Oklahoma,OK*	$ 5.56	*$1.38*
Hawaii,HI	*$ 5.98*	*$1.61*	*Oregon,OR*	*$24.63*	*$1.78*
Idaho,ID	*$10.96*	*$0.92*	*Pennsylv.,PA*	*$ 6.54*	**$0.00**
Illinois,IL	*$ 8.55*	**$0.41**	*Rhode Isl.,RI*	$ 3.75	*$1.84*
Indiana,IN	**$ 2.68**	$0.55	**South Car.,SC**	**$ 2.72**	**$0.12**
Iowa,IA	*$12.47*	*$1.01*	South Dak.,SD	$ 3.93	$0.81
Kansas,KS	**$ 2.50**	**$0.23**	**Tennessee,TN**	$ 4.40	**$0.15**
Kentucky,KY	**$ 1.92**	**$0.19**	*Texas,TX*	**$ 2.40**	*$1.39*
Louisiana,LA	**$ 2.50**	$0.46	*Utah,UT*	*$11.41*	*$1.56*
Maine,ME	$ 5.21	*$2.02*	*Vermont,VT*	**$ 0.68**	*$2.24*
Maryland,MD	**$ 1.50**	**$0.35**	*Virginia,VA*	*$20.13*	**$0.15**
Mass.,MA	$ 4.05	*$2.07*	*Washington,WA*	*$26.45*	*$2.15*
Michigan,MI	*$10.91*	*$0.74*	**West Virg.,WV**	**$ 1.85**	**$0.16**
Minnesota,MN	$ 5.03	*$1.61*	*Wisconsin,WI*	$ 3.25	*$2.30*
Mississippi,MS	*$ 6.75*	**$0.35**	**Wyoming, WY**	**$ 0.00**	$0.51
Missouri,MO	**$ 2.00**	**$0.23**	**Washington DC**	**$ 1.50**	$0.64
Montana,MT	$ 8.62	$0.72	AVERAGE	$ 6.35	$0.90

- **Bold:** Less than half the national average. States listed in **Bold** have a combined liquor and smokeless tobacco tax that is lower than the national average.

- *Italic:* More than half the national average. States listed in *Italics* have a combined liquor and smokeless tobacco tax that is higher than the national average.

*These statistics were compiled late one night after a drunken binge. They may or may not be correct, so don't do anything drastic like sell your home and move to Iowa because this chart shows it to have lower taxes than the state you live in.

The Snuff Box

By Simon Handelsman

A Menagerie of Snuff Boxes

Many of the modern, wooden snuff boxes currently available are rectangular with sliding lids. The wooden boxes from the 19th century are mainly round with lift off lids or rectangular with hinged lids. Many were ornamented with paintings, pressed designs, metal medallions or highly detailed drawings in pen and ink. But, one of the best qualities of wood is the ability to be shaped and carved. Men still sit and whittle everything from clothespin dolls and to the ends of handles to fit into the sockets of metal tools. Some of the most interesting snuffs are those that, under the hand of a master's knife, have become delightful shapes.

This lion snuffbox is a different beast. Although it is customary to classify recumbent lions as English, the lion symbol is shared by many European countries. Actually, the lion is an important symbol in nearly every culture on earth.

The cover has raised carvings of the Implements of the Passion which are reminders of the crucifixion, suffering and redemption. The lion can be thought of as the Lion of Judah and the wall against which he rests as the walls of Jerusalem. Specific interpretation of any object becomes speculation when there is little to place the box in a time frame or location. But, speculation is also harmless and pleasurable to consider.

What we know is that the box is fruitwood, carved by an accomplished craftsman, which leads to the conclusion that the folk art quality of the lion is purposeful. In fact, there are similar looking lion boxes made in silver.

Another box from the menagerie is the kneeling horse. Made from a light colored wood, this box is reminiscent of the Swedish Dala horse which is brightly painted with reins and saddle rendered in a highly stylized manner. This snuff has the reins carved free from the muzzle to the neck. The inscribed functional details of the saddle, cinch, stirrups and saddle bags are artfully mixed into the tree of life folk art decoration. The saddle lifts as a lid to the cavity within the body.

There is a long tradition of making these horses by lumberjacks, woodworkers and soldiers for over 300 years. They are thought to symbolize home and peace. This example is probably from the early 19th century and is delightful in the hand.

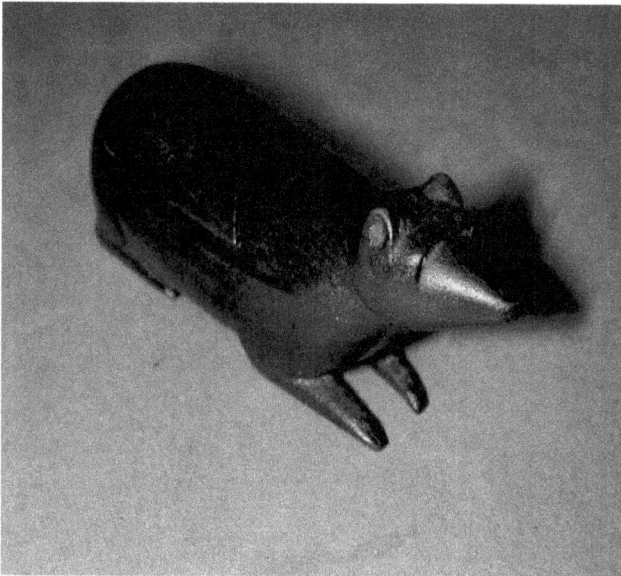
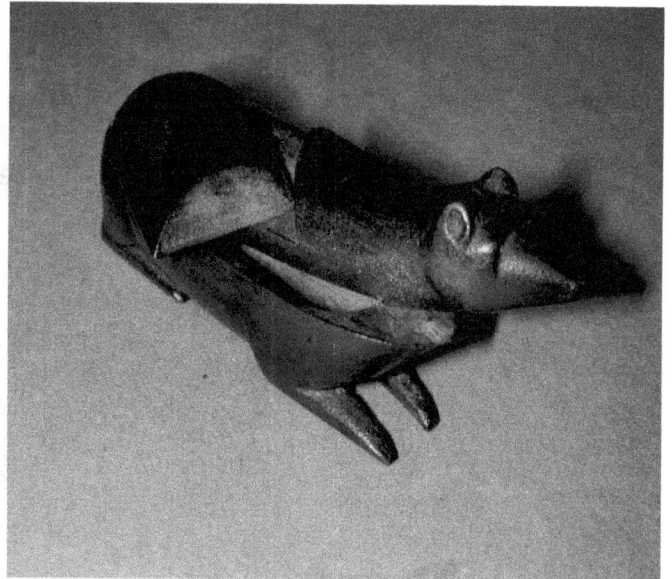

It is difficult to tell whether this charming fellow is a weasel, stoat or badger. His missing tail, which may have been a brush to flick away the stray grains of snuff, would have been helpful. He also works as a pivoting lid sailor's puzzle. The keystone at his throat has been broken and should be left as is but the box would be improved by adding some bristles as a tail. He appears to be waiting his owner's return for another pinch.

Frogs are a good shape for a snuff box. By placing the lid in the flat bottom, the hump of the back allows for a good size cavity for the snuff and a convenient shape for the palm to cup. This large fellow, 5 inches, is covered all over in chip carving. The lines of carving flow out from the tail like a chevron over the back. The eyes are black glass. The lid slides out parallel to the base and has one end carved to match the contours of the back legs and tail. Hard to keep your hands off this guy. No danger of warts.

The snuff box below is a stylized monkey, perhaps carved by someone who had never seen the animal in life. This carving with the ridge nose, long muzzle and huge eyes is a sort of lemur-baboon mix. The monkey has glass eyes and bone teeth and is carved from Mahogany. The lid is set on the extreme back of the head with a small metal oval insert near the top to serve as an aid to opening and a tiny hinge at the base. If the box is held face down, the shape fits into the web formed by the thumb and forefinger perfectly! The ears may even act as a carved ridge to help the grip. The feel in either hand is too good to be just coincidence.

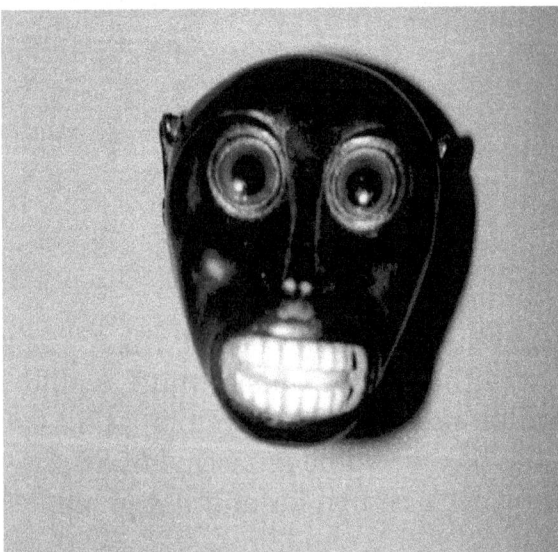

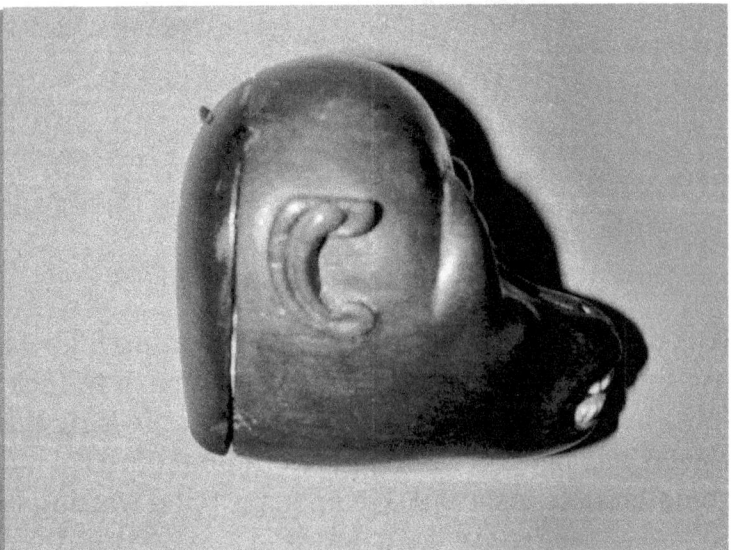

This ebony wood ape enjoys the same good ergonomics. However, his visage is more realistic and less welcoming. The face is smooth with a realistic nose and glass eyes. The eyes are deeply set and follow you as the snuff box is moved. The hair is curly on top of the head and straight along the sides. The teeth are bone with large canines. Much rarer than his monkey cousin.

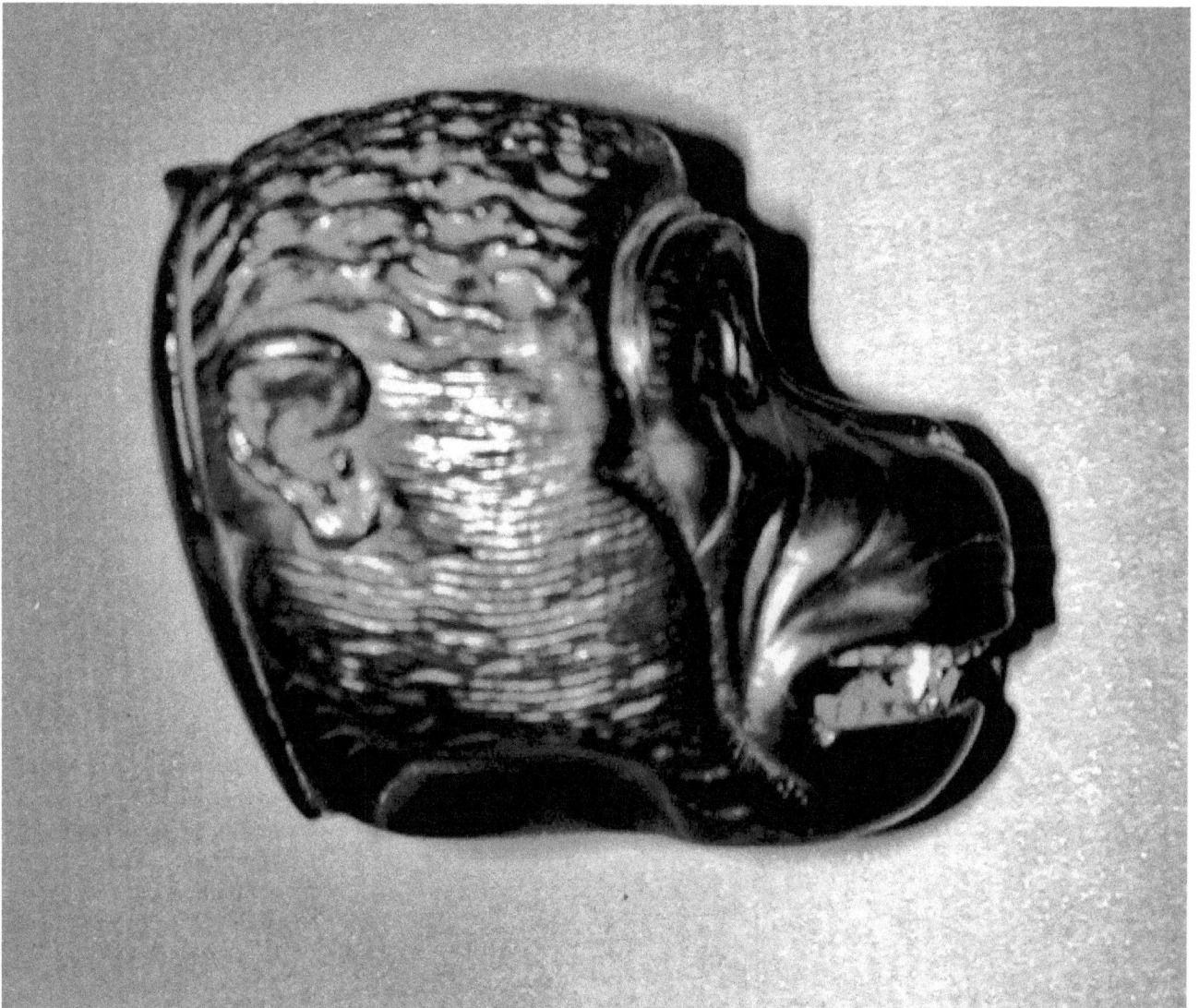

Often, the artisans of the 18th century worked from published engravings or more likely, a hand drawn copy of the engraving. Why buy an expensive book when you could visit a friendly print shop and trace or draw your own copy of the figure you needed? In fact, print makers themselves usually worked from other prints. As George Washington became famous during the American revolution, no one in Europe knew what he looked like. Some early images appear to be totally made up. Later images improved in accuracy as more prints copied from actual paintings of the man circulated. Modern Americans recognize Washington more from his image on currency than from contemporary paintings.

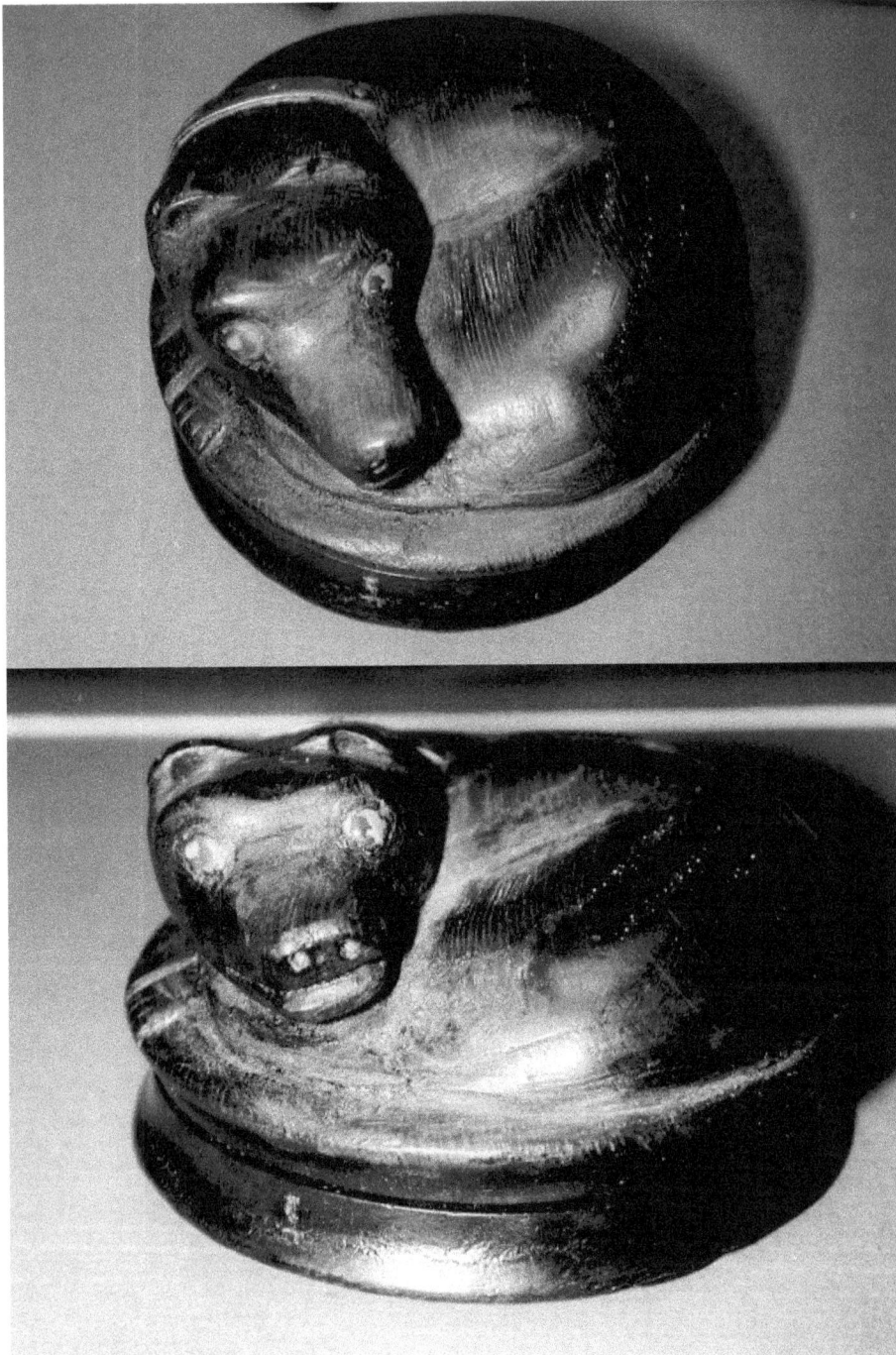

This last box, with man's best friend curled up on the cover, is fairly unique. The dog has a copper collar fastened to his neck by tiny copper nails with heads that look like studs on the collar.

Examining the profile of the box reveals that the bottom has a finely turned, rimmed edge while the top has a thick, less uniform edge. It is likely that the owner carved a top with his dog on it and fitted the new top to an old bottom. Some care was taken to make the wood grain look like markings in the fur. A fine piece of folk art.   STE

Simon Handelsman is one of the world's foremost authorities on antique snuff boxes. Visit his website at www.snuffbox.com for more information about vintage snuff paraphernalia.

Parting Shot:

"I would rather receive a nod from an American than a snuff box from an emperor."

-Lord Byron

CRUSHED ICE XtraStrong Mint by: NICK AND JOHNNY

www.snuscentral.com

www.facebook.com/snuscentral

WARNING: Smokeless tobacco is addictive.

Steven Lull has been rocking out in local bands for the last thirty years.

He's cut a couple of demos. Played all the clubs. Even opened up for Coal Chamber once.

But Steve's in his late 40's now, and he's been divorced twice. His current bandmates are in college. Steve works part time at the bookstore in order to keep his utilities turned on.

Right now he's in the middle of a Led Zeppelin cover. But after tonight's gig, Steve is going to stop by the Quik Mart and purchase a can of snuff and a Red Bull.

And this evening, while he's sitting alone in his kitchen, he's going to roll that snuff can back and forth between his fingers. Thinking about his past. Thinking about his future.

And right before he pulls the trigger and sends a .38 slug into his brain, he's going to smile. Because even though the music industry may have failed him, his snuff has never let him down.

And that, my friends, is *true* Rock and Roll.

Steven Lull was a snuff taker.

The Ephemeris was his magazine.

www.ingramcontent.com/pod-product-compliance
Lightning Source LLC
Chambersburg PA
CBHW081543040426
42448CB00015B/3201